globalize it!

globalize it!

the stories of the IMF, the World Bank, the WTO—and those who protest

Brendan January

Twenty-First Century Books
Brookfield, Connecticut

Cover photograph courtesy of © Paul Schulenburg/Images.com, Inc.
Photographs courtesy of Corbis: pp. 2-3 (© AFP), 10 (© Reuters
NewMedia, Inc.), 54 (© AFP); The Image Works: pp. 13 (© Steven Rubin),
16 (© Steven Rubin), 31 (© Mark Reinstein); Corbis/Sygma: p. 15 (© Le
Segretain Pascal); Getty Images: pp. 18 (© Forrest Anderson/Liaison), 23
(Hulton/Archive), 25 (Hulton/Archive), 36 (© Francis Li/Liaison), 63 (©
Forrest Anderson), 73 (© Spencer Platt), 119; Gamma Presse: pp. 48, 66,
112; Sipa Press: p. 59 (© Thomas Haley); AP/Wide World Photos: pp. 72,
101, 123. Maps by Joe LeMonnier.

Library of Congress Cataloging-in-Publication Data
January, Brendan, 1972–
Globalize it! : the stories of the IMF, the World Bank, the WTO, and those
who protest / Brendan January.
v. cm.
Includes bibliographical references and index.
Contents: The battle of Seattle—A world order : the foundations of globalization—I don't want to be like Mike— Globalization is good for the
globe—Killing the world to save it?—Whose culture?—Protest—The IMF
faces a meltdown : economic crisis in Mexico, Russia, and Asia —
Mistakes and resolve — A new world.
ISBN 0-7613-2417-8 (lib. bdg.)
1. International economic integration—Juvenile literature.
2. Globalization—Juvenile literature. 3. Free trade—Juvenile literature.
4. International business enterprises—Juvenile literature. 5. International
finance—Juvenile literature. 6. Equality—Juvenile literature. 7. World
Bank. 8. International Monetary Fund. 9. World Trade Organization.
[1. Globalization. 2. Free trade. 3. International business enterprises.
4. International finance. 5. World Bank. 6. International Monetary Fund.
7. World Trade Organization.] I. Title.
HF1418.5 .J363 2003   337—dc21   2002152509

Published by Twenty-First Century Books
A Division of The Millbrook Press, Inc.
2 Old New Milford Road
Brookfield, Connecticut 06804
www.millbrookpress.net

Contents

globalize it!

EUROPE

ASIA

AFRICA

SOUTH
ATLANTIC
OCEAN

INDIAN
OCEAN

AUSTRALIA

This map shows the wealthiest, most industrialized areas in the world (gray), and the areas of the world that are in various stages of development (white).

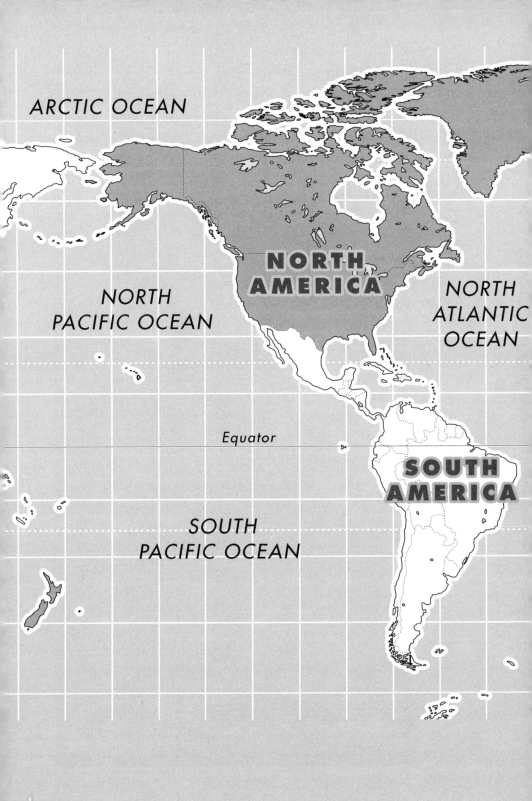

ARCTIC OCEAN

NORTH
AMERICA

NORTH
PACIFIC OCEAN

NORTH
ATLANTIC
OCEAN

Equator

SOUTH
AMERICA

SOUTH
PACIFIC OCEAN

The Battle of Seattle began as a peaceful demonstration that filled the downtown streets with protestors who carried homemade signs, banners, and flags decrying the disparities of the World Trade Organization.

The Battle of Seattle

At dawn on November 30, 1999, the streets of Seattle, Washington, exploded in protest. Tens of thousands filled the city's downtown, marching, chanting, blocking traffic, forming human chains, and performing theater.

Representatives of every political persuasion seemed to be in the swirling mix of people—college students, Communists, teachers, animal-rights groups, farmers, nursing students, vegetarians, electrical and steel workers, and common citizens. Representatives of the American Federation of Teachers thundered by on Harley Davidson motorcycles. A group of women calling themselves the "Vegan Dykes" marched topless. Another group decried the despoiling of the rain forests.[1]

Out of the mass of people and causes emerged a powerful consensus—we don't like the way the world is being run. Powerful, rich corporations have become masters of the world, shouted demonstrators. They have eclipsed local governments and workers' rights, undermined democracy, and destroyed the environment.

"I don't believe we should have the corporations ruining the world," an eighty-two-year-old woman told a reporter. Filled with concern, the woman had flown to Seattle from Concord, Massachusetts, to join the protest.

Bill Guthrie, a twenty-eight-year-old pipe fitter from San Jose, California, told the same reporter that he was astounded so many different people could rally around one cause. "But it's not an issue of left or right," he added. "It's an issue of top and bottom."[2]

The protesters had not gathered in Seattle on their own initiative. They had been drawn there. Many of the people who controlled the world, or who the protesters believed controlled the world, were already in the city. Delegates, journalists, and corporate heads from more than one hundred countries were attending a meeting of the World Trade Organization (WTO). The WTO is a group of more than 140 nations that debates and establishes rules of trade among its members—behind closed doors.

It seemed to be a good time for the WTO, because the global economy was booming. The United States was enjoying the longest uninterrupted economic expansion in peacetime. Investors had poured trillions of dollars into the stock market and pushed it to record heights. A new high-technology industry had arisen, fueled by the enormous use of computers and the Internet. Pundits and analysts spoke with excitement about a new economy that defied traditional laws of business growth, inflation, and recession.

Seattle itself had done well in the economic boom. The elegant city, with its distinctive Space Needle gracing the skyline, was known around the world as the home of computer software giant Microsoft and its billionaire founder, Bill Gates. In the damp Seattle climate, many residents drank cups of steaming coffee purchased at Starbucks, a chain that had opened stores across the United States and in several other countries.

If the future was coming, it seemed to arrive in Seattle first. That was also true at the 1999 WTO meeting. Two visions of the world were clashing in the city's avenues.

Crowds surrounded the Paramount Theater, where the WTO talks were scheduled to open. Organized protesters

During the protest march, some groups performed open-air plays to portray the evils of corporations.

formed human barriers, using hollow pipes to link their arms in a chain of limbs that police could not break. Trade delegates were blocked from the theater, and their limousines stood idle. U.S. Secretary of State Madeleine Albright and U.N. Secretary-General Kofi Annan never left their hotels.

The WTO opening ceremonies were postponed.

Adrenaline surged in the streets after this victory. To the pounding of drums and the ecstatic cheers, the demonstrations continued. More than 20,000 workers from the AFL-CIO, the largest labor union in North America, marched to object to the thousands of American jobs sent overseas.

That evening, another protest group showed up in the downtown area, smashing windows and spray-painting walls. Long dark lines of police appeared and arrested more than twenty people. At 5 P.M., the governor of Washington declared a state of emergency.

The next day, city police and national guardsmen cleared the streets. No longer were protestors allowed to roam at will. When demonstrators clogged intersections in a bid to prevent delegates from attending meetings, police arrested more than four hundred of them. To break down communications among the protesters, police grabbed cell phones. That night, police fired tear gas canisters, and the stinging clouds drifted around the hotel where President Bill Clinton was staying. The crowds finally began to break up. The police had confiscated gas masks.[3]

The next day, the WTO delegates were able to meet successfully. Seattle's downtown was shuttered, its empty streets littered with broken glass. The protesters had clearly made their point.

In the evening, a group wearing dark clothes and hoods rampaged through the downtown area. They smashed the windows of a Starbucks coffee shop and spray-painted the symbol of the international anarchy movement on building walls.

"What they are telling us in the streets is that this is an issue we've been silent on," President Clinton told trade representatives. "And we won't be silent anymore. . . . The sooner the WTO opens up the process, we'll see less demonstrations and more constructive debate."

"If the WTO expects to have public support grow for our endeavors, the public must see and hear and, in a very real sense, actually join in the deliberations," Clinton told another group at a lunch meeting. "That's the only way they can know the process is fair, and know their concerns were at least considered."4

Riot police were called in to crack down on the anti-WTO demonstrations in Seattle.

After several frustrating days, the trade talks collapsed in failure. In a foul mood, the trade delegates abandoned the city. The reporters and protesters soon followed. Exhausted Seattle residents returned to work.

But the protesters weren't finished. Adding insult to injury, a group managed to break into an electrical center next door to the WTO's headquarters in Geneva, Switzerland. They cut off power, and for forty-five minutes, the lights and computer screens of the organization went dark.

In contrast to the somber mood at the WTO, jubilant activists were thrilled to have seized the world's attention. Colorful images of rioting protesters, shattered Seattle storefronts, and rows of police clad in riot gear filled newscasts and the front pages of newspapers and magazines. The "Battle of Seattle," as it was described by excited activists, had changed the world.

For many Americans, the 1990s were a quiet time of uninterrupted prosperity and contentment. Crime was dropping and salaries were rising. What could be wrong? But the graphic news footage of scenes of fury and violence in Seattle shocked Americans. It forced them to take a closer look at the world and consider the issues raised by the protesters.

Within days, a term became commonly used in the media, in schools, and around the water coolers where workers stopped to talk and gossip. It was a word that described the immense changes transforming the Earth—globalization.

What Is Globalization?

The evidence of globalization is everywhere. Europeans and Americans wear clothes made in Honduras, drive automobiles manufactured in Japan, and sip wine from Australia. Africans organize Western-style elections and surf the Internet with American-designed software. The grandchildren of a tribal chief in Indonesia, clad in matching Pokemon outfits, chase each other through their village. In China and Japan, people line up outside their local KFC. Disney is everywhere.

Such an immense exchange of goods, people, and ideas has never occurred before in history. Languages, cul-

Globalization is manifested in the thousands of McDonald's that have opened in countries around the world. In 1992, China's first McDonald's was opened in the busiest shopping district of Beijing, the capital city.

tures, religions, values, and peoples are mixing, clashing, and blending together.

It's globalization—a brave, exhilarating new world of exciting and terrifying change. It is economic, political, and social. It's here and more of it is coming.

In the past ten years, the world has shrunk, bound by an ever-tightening web of communication and transportation. Billions of bits of data are sent every second around the globe. Airplanes crowd the skies and runways. Cargo ships, heavily loaded with goods, steam into and out of the world's ports daily.

Globalization will bring change and affect every decision—from how Congress votes to a shopper's choice of fruit. It will affect the air you breathe, the food you eat, and the water you drink. It regulates the car you drive, the job you work at, and how much you're paid. It will influence how your children and grandchildren live, whether they will prosper, stagnate, or fall into poverty.

The effects of globalization can already be seen. It has lifted entire societies out of squalor in Asia. It has driven thousands off farms and into the crowded, teeming cities of Latin America. It has created jobs and at the same time forced down wages. It has created a global culture that can be beamed onto any household television in the world. It has eased the spread of the AIDS virus.

It has become the question of our times: Is globalization the problem or is it the solution?

Many people answer loudly, "the solution!" They include factory workers who can enjoy middle-class luxuries for the first time. They include those who point out that the free flow of trade and ideas generates wealth.

WHEN DID GLOBALIZATION BEGIN?

Just when globalization started is an ongoing argument. Some date it to Columbus's voyage in 1492, when he saw a jade-green coast rising up out of the Atlantic Ocean and called it the Indies. He had actually landed in the Americas, and his voyage led to the first global exchange of goods among Europe, Asia, Africa, and the Americas.

Others say it originated in the 1800s, when parts of the world began industrializing and exchanging huge amounts of goods. Still others argue it arrived in the twentieth century, when the first international economic organizations were founded.

Whatever the arguments, most agree that this period of globalization is unique in its extensive reach to all areas in the world. As Thomas Friedman put it, "the world is ten years old."[5]

People are living longer, healthier lives. They have better access to education and to the world of ideas.

But to many others, globalization is the problem. They cite the fact that more than 3 billion people live on less than $2 a day, and 1.3 billion have no source of clean water. They point out that the problem is not going to get any easier. The United Nations predicts that the world population will reach 9.3 billion in 2050. Almost half will be hungry.

Globalization, say activists and critics, is creating a new and vast divide between those who live in wealth and those who live in poverty. The world's poor glimpse images of the prosperous world, distant but also an intimate presence on television screens. They see shiny automobiles, huge green lawns, and smiles of perfect white teeth. It's a world that seems to care little for their health, their values, or their dreams.

That seeming indifference has fueled rage, the bitter frustrations of societies, the fury of the laid-off and exploited worker, and the anger in the slum cities where the profits of the new economy never seem to arrive.

This book looks at how globalization is transforming how we see our work, our environment, and each other. It will present the arguments both for and against the process, and explore the passion behind the issues.

To understand globalization, we must look back to a world far more divided than today. The founding of modern globalization took place more than fifty years ago, in the wake of the most devastating war the world had ever seen.

chapter two

A World Order
The Foundations
of Globalization

As World War II drew to a close in the mid-1940s, global leaders surveyed the world in shock and horror. Never before had so much energy and so many lives been consumed by war. The cities of Europe and Japan had been devastated by fleets of bombers. Millions of soldiers and civilians had been slaughtered or scattered from their homes. France had been conquered and occupied. Great Britain was exhausted.

Never again, they said, will we make the mistakes that cause war—the kind of mistakes that were made after World War I ended in 1918. At that time, harsh terms were imposed on defeated Germany. The peace treaty helped destabilize the world economy and caused a crushing depression. Lines of hungry people waiting for bread snaked through city streets in Europe and the United States. In Germany, prices of goods skyrocketed. To buy a loaf of bread or a coat took stacks of money. German soldiers who had lost arms and legs in the war were left with worthless pensions and were forced to put out begging

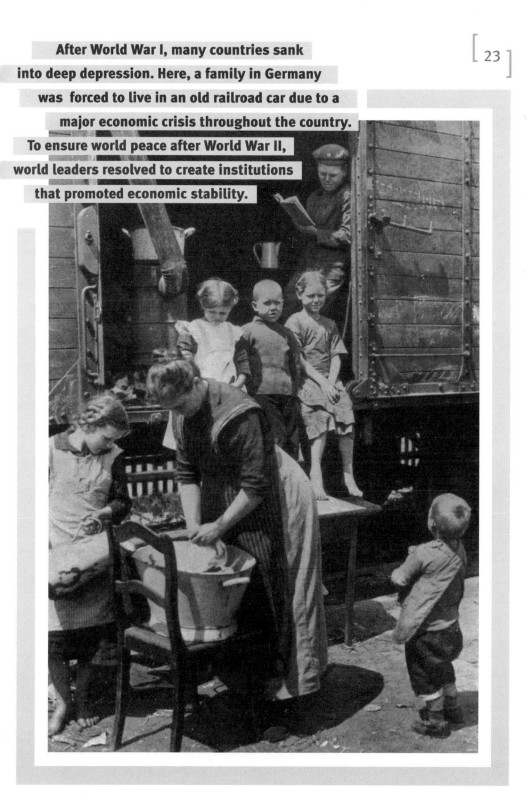

After World War I, many countries sank into deep depression. Here, a family in Germany was forced to live in an old railroad car due to a major economic crisis throughout the country. To ensure world peace after World War II, world leaders resolved to create institutions that promoted economic stability.

bowls. Angry, fanatic leaders thrived, feeding off the discontent of the unemployed, the hopeless, and the bitter.

Never again. To ensure peace, the world's leaders came together at the end of World War II to form the United Nations (UN), a place where countries could resolve their differences with words rather than with bullets. But the delegates also knew that lack of money, food, and hope would lead only to more conflict. They promised to help each other economically.

With this in mind, delegates created institutions to promote economic stability. They wanted to avoid depressions and ruinous economic policies. Countries that grow rich together, they reasoned, will have less reason to fight each other.

Bretton Woods and GATT

To start, nations needed stable money. Today, people exchange billions of paper bills every day to buy the things they need. Most never realize that without a government guarantee, the bills are no more valuable than tissue paper or play money. And during World War II, most governments had been shattered or severely weakened.

In Europe, no one wanted to sell important items—such as potatoes or firewood—for a strip of paper that might be worthless. But without money, the economies would be strangled.

In 1944, at Bretton Woods, New Hampshire, government representatives agreed to base their paper money on the strongest currency in the world at that time—the U.S. dollar. Governments guaranteed that they would exchange dollars for their currencies at a set price. This inspired con-

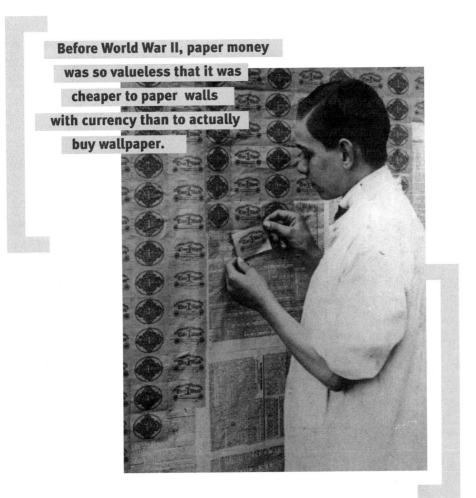

Before World War II, paper money was so valueless that it was cheaper to paper walls with currency than to actually buy wallpaper.

fidence over the next few years. Germans, for example, knew that their mark would always be worth a certain amount of dollars. Soon, Germans were able to use their money to buy goods, save, and invest. The economy began to grow.

Another agreement reached at Bretton Woods was to promote trade. Trade—or the exchange of goods between nations—brought prosperity. The delegates were especially worried about protectionism. When a country is protectionist, it tries to insulate its own industries from the outside world. The government sets high taxes, called tariffs, on incoming goods. The result is often a trade war, as nations set higher and higher tariffs in retaliation. This leads to a collapse in trade, prices soar, and nations wall themselves off. These policies helped create and sustain the Great Depression in the 1930s.

To set trade agreements, the nations formed the General Agreement on Tariffs and Trade (GATT). Established in 1948 by the United States and twenty-two other Western countries, GATT agreed not to resort to protectionism. Instead, GATT held several "rounds," in which delegates reached broad agreements to reduce tariffs. Tariff rates on industrial goods were reduced from 40 percent in 1947 to 5 percent in 1994. In 1995, GATT was replaced by the WTO.

World leaders didn't stop with the creation of GATT and the UN. They also wanted to stabilize currency exchange rates—or the prices at which countries exchange money. For example, when an American buys a Japanese car, the American pays dollars. Later, the dollars are exchanged by the Japanese company into the money of Japan, called the yen. It is in everyone's best interests that the rate at which the dollar and the yen are exchanged stays basically stable. That way, the American gets a good car, and the Japanese company knows it is getting paid in money that has value. Everyone wins.

To oversee these rates, world leaders founded the International Monetary Fund (IMF). They also founded the World Bank, an organization charged with providing loans to poor countries. These two organizations, so critical to globalization, will get more attention later in the chapter.

The Cold War

At first, the policies of the IMF, the World Bank, and GATT received scant public attention. From the 1950s to the 1980s, the world was divided by the Cold War, a period when the United States and the Soviet Union competed to dominate the world.

The two countries represented two views of how politics and economies should be organized and run. In broad terms, the United States and Western Europe favored the free market. The free market is the result of millions of individuals making millions of decisions every day. If a factory makes a coat that no one buys, the company changes its style or goes out of business.

Companies and corporations dominate the free market. They strive to produce as many goods as cheaply as possible.

"Our system freed the individual genius of man. Released him to fly as high and as far as his own talent and energy would take him," said Ronald Reagan in a radio address in 1976. "We allocate resources not by government decision but by the millions of decisions customers make when they go into the market place to buy. If something seems too high-priced we buy something else. Thus resources are steered toward those things the people want most at the price they are willing to pay. It may not be a perfect system but it's better than any other that's ever been tried."

The Communist Soviet Union believed the economy could be planned and run, thus eliminating the cruelties and inefficiencies of the market. Economists and government leaders would decide how many cars to build, how much wheat to grow, how many refrigerators to manufacture. Consumers have a smaller role in the Communist economy than in the free market.

The battle between free market capitalism and communism became a fierce competition for the hearts and minds of the world. Europe was divided by what English leader Winston Churchill called the Iron Curtain, which followed the borders of East Germany, Czechoslovakia, Hungary, and Yugoslavia. The border was tightly sealed, with giant armies glaring at each other across barbed wire. American armies fought in Korea and Vietnam. The Soviets supported rebels in Latin America and Africa and invaded Afghanistan.

Each side bitterly criticized the other. Americans attacked socialism, saying it was brutal, repressive, and made workers lazy and indifferent. The Soviets ridiculed how American politicians bought elections, and how the rich drove luxury automobiles past filthy slums teeming with the unemployed.

The two sides competed against each other for four decades. But by the end of the 1980s, the Soviet Union's economy was on the verge of collapse. Unable to sustain its armies, the Soviets withdrew from Eastern Europe, an area it had dominated since the end of World War II. The Iron Curtain was abruptly torn down and the Cold War was over.

A New World Order

Globalization grew out of the rubble of the Cold War. One of the greatest struggles in world history, between socialism and capitalism, had been decisively won and the results were clear—the free market, not communism, was the best way to organize an economy.

This victory became even more obvious after curious Westerners began visiting the former Communist countries. For many, it was their first time examining socialism up close. It looked terrible.

Eager and excited West Germans drove over the border into East Germany after the Berlin Wall fell in 1989. They were shocked at what they saw: shabby homes, potholes, and pollution. The tiny, boxlike East German automobile, called the Trabi, looked absurd next to the sleek Mercedes automobiles driven by the West Germans.

When the Cold War raged between the United States and the Soviet Union, pitting free market capitalism against state-run socialism, the world's nations could appeal to Socialist principals as they managed their economies. No longer. The rule of the market was king.

Leave the economy to the experts, to private enterprise, to the investors with capital, and to the Wall Street analysts that manage it for them. The free market and its philosophy of open trade had triumphed. Americans boasted that their system was the formula for peace and prosperity, and they were determined to use the IMF, the World Bank, and free trade to spread those ideals to the rest of the world.

Journalist and commentator P. J. O'Rourke captured this confident attitude in a column about the end of the Cold War: "In the end we beat them with Levi 501 jeans," he wrote. "Seventy-two years of communist indoctrination and propaganda was drowned out by a three-ounce Sony Walkman. A huge totalitarian system with all its tanks and guns, gulag camps and secret police has been brought to its knees because nobody wants to wear Bulgarian shoes.

They may have had the soldiers and the warheads and the fine sounding ideology that suckered the college students and nitwit Third Worlders, but we had all the fun. Now they're lunch, and we're number one on the planet."[1]

American leaders pushed other nations to lower trade barriers, knitting countries together through a prosperous exchange of goods. The IMF, the World Bank, and free trade became, or were perceived as, the instruments of this formula.

The IMF and the World Bank in the 1990s

By the 1990s, the IMF had become the doctor that fixed ailing economies. Based in Washington, D.C., the IMF can quickly lend billions of dollars to a country's banking system or government. But the IMF's medicine can be bitter. As a condition of the loan, the IMF demands changes in how the country's economy is run. These changes can be painful, especially in the short term.

The IMF's sister institution, the World Bank, is located just across the street from the IMF in Washington, D.C. The World Bank uses the backing of its member countries, mostly the richest nations, to borrow money. The bank then lends the money to countries that are too poor to get loans from other banks.

The World Bank has sponsored many projects over the past fifty years. In the 1960s and 1970s, it tried to eliminate poverty by building up countries' infrastructures—giant dams, roads, power plants, and irrigation systems. More recently, the bank has attacked poverty by funding schools, hospitals, and family planning programs.

The World Bank headquarters in Washington, D.C.

The World Bank, which has a staff of more than nine thousand, has given loans to more than one hundred countries. In 2000, the World Bank lent $15.3 billion for specific projects. According to its Web site, the bank uses "finance and ideas to improve living standards and eliminate the worst forms of poverty," and claims the "main focus is on helping the poorest people and the poorest countries."[2]

The supporters of the IMF and World Bank describe them as pillars of a stable, prosperous global economy. Free trade reduces barriers and increases the exchange of goods, resulting in cheaper products and more jobs. The IMF helps save economies from bankruptcy and the collapse of currency that can devastate a nation. It provides the sound advice and reforms necessary to flourish in the global economy. The World Bank provides loans for projects that provide jobs and raise the standard of living.

Who could argue with that?

The Backlash

A lot of people. Free trade, the IMF, and World Bank have become the targets of violent, angry protests like the ones in Seattle. The backlash against globalization is growing, a reaction against the world these three institutions champion—a take-no-prisoners type of capitalism that seems to leave little space for individuals, their cares, and their dreams.

To the protesters, globalization is by the rich, of the rich, and for the rich. It pits the wealthy nations of the North—North America, Europe, and Japan—against the poor, developing nations of the South—essentially everybody else.

This struggle, say protesters, is not just against the World Bank, the IMF, and the WTO, it is against a culture of greed and profit. In these terms, those organizations are just puppets for another force, one far more powerful and deadly—the transnational corporation.

To the protesters, the transnational corporations—corporations that operate in several countries—are the true enemy. They build unsafe factories, pay workers poverty wages, and pillage the environment to satisfy their greed. With their staggering wealth, they can bribe local officials and buy politicians. With their obnoxious, omnipresent advertising campaigns, they destroy cultures and degrade public space.

Transnational corporations and their products are everywhere. Just look down. In any classroom or gym in the United States, chances are that someone is wearing Nike sneakers. You may even have a pair stored in your locker. Nike was one of the first true modern transnational corporations. It profited tremendously from globalization, but its success has also made it one of the largest targets of antiglobalization protesters.

chapter three
I Don't Want to Be Like Mike

In the early 1960s, a young Oregonian named Phil Knight began driving to track meets and selling sneakers out of the back of his car. As a student at Stanford Business School in California, Knight had written a paper suggesting that importing cheap but well-made running shoes from Japan into the United States would result in record profits.

His theory proved correct. Shoe sales were strong, and within five years Knight and a partner decided to launch their own company. Knight named the company Nike, after the Greek goddess of victory. Knight also paid $35 for a brand symbol for his shoe—a flat checkmark drawn by a Portland State University design student.

"I don't love it," Knight told her at the time, "but maybe it'll grow on me."

The Nike "Swoosh" was born.[1] By the 1980s, Nike annual sales had jumped from $10 million to more than $250 million.

As Knight had first outlined in his business paper, Nike's headquarters and most of its customers were in the

United States. But the factories and workers who made the shoes were scattered around the world. Nike was a company without borders—a transnational corporation.

Factories Go Abroad

Nike was not alone. Large companies, especially in the United States and Europe, had begun manufacturing goods overseas in poor countries lumped together under the name Third World.

The name Third World once applied to those nations that decided to stay neutral during the Cold War. But it also came to mean poor and undeveloped countries. Today, many activists refer to those countries collectively as the "South." Economists and politicians have also called them "developing countries."

Until the 1970s, Third World economies struggled. They exported raw materials such as timber, precious metals, and oil, and imported manufactured goods that few of their citizens could afford. Rising birth rates put enormous pressure on society. Planters cleared forests to grow food. Thousands migrated to the cities in search of work. There, they joined millions in squalid shantytown slums with little access to schools or hospitals.

Though labor was extremely cheap, few Western nations built factories in the Third World. Company executives believed that social and cultural barriers, as well as the difficulty of operating in a foreign country, were too much to overcome.

But in the 1970s many Third World nations began a transformation. For various reasons—including better communications and price pressures—major corporations began moving factories to the Third World. Countries that once sold only raw materials began exporting manufactured goods such as Nike running shoes.

Some countries, such as Korea and Taiwan, benefited enormously. The steady factory work and pay created a middle class that began buying goods—such as refrigerators, cars, television sets, and homes. Even more jobs were created. In South Korea, the hourly wage in 1975 was just 5 percent of the American hourly wage. In 1996, it was 46 percent.[2]

But the transformation came with a price. With growing profits and labor forces, these transnational corporations began exercising a power and influence they had not

Nike is a transnational corporation, which means that it has factories around the world, including in Third World nations. The one shown here is in China.

had before. Nike's budget and profits made it richer than many countries. And transnational corporations were also not ashamed to promote their interests by pressing for local environmental and labor laws that helped protect their profits. In the face of such pressure, many governments were too corrupt or too small to resist them.

By the 1990s the corporations had grown to tremendous size and strength. In 1999, the UN noted that fifty of the one hundred largest economies in the world were transnational companies. In 1997 the sales of General Motors, based in the United States, and Mitsubishi, based in Japan, were larger than the total wealth generated in several countries, including Greece, South Africa, Poland, and Israel. The combined revenues of the largest 200 corporations exceed that of 182 nations where 80 percent of the population lives.[3]

Transnational corporations and globalization go hand in hand. Transnational corporations have used innovations in communication and technology—digital satellites, the Internet—to spread their reach throughout the world and at the same time make the world a much smaller place.

These trends came together in the 1980s to create the first global superstar—Michael Jordan.

Michael Jordan and Nike Go Global

When Michael Jordan played in his first professional game with the Chicago Bulls in 1984, neither his team nor the National Basketball Association was doing well. Television viewers had stayed away, and the Bulls played in arenas dark with thousands of empty seats. Ten of the league's teams were either bankrupt or for sale.

Then came Michael. Displaying a combination of grace, speed, and an extraordinary instinct for defense, Jordan transformed the basketball court into his personal playground. Within two years, he was averaging more than thirty-seven points a game. His moves and intensity mesmerized crowds and opponents.

In the 1986 playoffs he sank two clutch foul shots after the final buzzer to win a game against the Boston Celtics. "I think he's god disguised as Michael Jordan," opponent Larry Bird said afterward.4

As Jordan dazzled, television viewership surged, and the Chicago Coliseum was suddenly sold out night after night to cheering crowds. In just two years, basketball was transformed from a moribund spectacle to the hottest sport in America.

Nike was also there to share in the success. In 1987, Knight paid Jordan $18 million over seven years to endorse Nike's "Air Jordan" sneakers. The image of Jordan, grinning and holding a pair of sneakers, seemed to be everywhere.

Nike founder Phil Knight used the tools of globalization to build an empire. Widespread satellite communication allowed Nike to beam Jordan all over the world. By the end of the 1980s, NBA games could be seen in more than one hundred countries. In Japan, teenagers told interviewers that their two most desired items were Coke and Air Jordans.5

Jordan's enormous popularity spread the Nike Swoosh and its slogan, "Just Do It." The success was astonishing. From 1987 to 1989, Nike sales doubled to a staggering $1.7 billion.

But there was one problem, and it wouldn't go away. No one denied that Jordan was extremely talented, worked hard, and was worth a great deal of money. But Michael earned more in one year from his shoe endorsements—$25 million—than the 25,000 workers in the Indonesian shoe industry combined did.

Some people began to notice this and, more importantly, they began to protest.

The Plight and the Fury of Workers

By the 1990s workers were willing to take their complaints directly to their bosses. In 1996, a Mexican named Juan Tovar Santos left his home in Acuña and traveled to Pittsburgh, Pennsylvania. Santos was employed at an Alcoa factory just inside Mexico, and he wanted to tell the heads of the company what it was like to work there. At the Alcoa shareholder meeting, Santos listened to a glowing report given by CEO Paul H. O'Neill, who spoke of record profits for the company. Then Santos took the microphone.

Using an interpreter, Santos described earning $6 a day and tyrannical managers who allowed workers only three sheets of toilet paper each when they used the bathrooms.

When gas leaked, more than one hundred workers became so ill that they were taken to hospitals.

O'Neill defended Alcoa and told the shareholders that the factories are "so clean they can eat off the floor."

"That's a lie!" Santos fired back.

The argument between the two men—one who earned less than $2,000 a year, the other more than $2 million—was not just between individuals.

In Acuña, the Alcoa factory was surrounded by slums. Along with the other, mostly American, companies in the region, Alcoa paid few taxes to the city. And it showed. Public services were poor, the schools underfunded, the sewage system overwhelmed. Of the 150,000 residents in the city, half of them did not have indoor plumbing.[6]

If an American company employed Americans in such conditions, it would be a national scandal.

The Story of a Factory

But that was part of the problem. Santos's job had once been American. The United States had grown into a powerful and prosperous nation by offering well-paying factory jobs that allowed workers to raise their living standards.

When those jobs were moved to other countries, as in Alcoa's case, they underwent a startling transformation.

To capture this change, reporter William Adler wrote about an American factory job as it was moved from its origin in Paterson, New Jersey, to locations in the southern states, and finally to Mexico.

Mollie James, a fifty-nine-year-old Paterson resident, had worked at a local factory—the Universal Manufacturing Company—for almost thirty-five years before it closed in June 1989. The factory specialized in manufacturing ballast for fluorescent lights.

With the union wages she earned at the factory, James made about $30,000 a year. "She also received company-paid health insurance," wrote Adler in *Mollie's Job*, "and the peace of mind that came from a secure job—a job she could raise a family on, buy a house, a car, borrow money against, count on for her future."[7]

But in the late 1980s, MagneTek, a business based in Los Angeles, purchased Universal. No longer content with just making profits, the corporate heads wanted to make huge profits. They planned to move the factory to southern states, where labor was cheaper. Eventually, the factories would end up in Mexico, where labor was cheapest of all.

When James came in to work, she noticed vacant spots on the factory floor where whole pieces of machinery had been ripped up and shipped south. In June 1988 the factory—with some of same pieces taken from Paterson—opened in Matamoros, Mexico, just across the border from Texas. For thousands of Mexicans desperate to escape poverty, working in the factory was considered a dream job.

But Adler describes a very disturbing transformation that has occurred to "Mollie's job" as it moves farther and farther south. It no longer pays the benefits that it did in Paterson.

Instead, a young woman named Balbina Duque works for MagneTek at the same position. She earns about $50 a week, or $2,500 a year. With that paycheck, she and her three children can live in a concrete block shack with a corrugated roof within sight of the factory. Balbina shares two rooms with her sister, who has two children of her own. A single lightbulb, dangling from the ceiling, illuminates both rooms. Outside, the families share an outhouse and a single spigot of water.[8]

The corporations in the area pay few taxes, and so the town is mired in poverty, with few hospitals, schools, or sewage systems.

Political leaders raged at their inability to stop the movement of jobs to areas with cheaper workers. New York Democrat John LaFalce headed a congressional committee that discovered that U.S. tax dollars paid for conferences that encouraged corporations to move jobs from the United States to Mexico. LaFalce had seen thousands of factory jobs leave his district, leaving laid-off workers and devastated families and communities. LaFalce expressed his frustration over a corporate attitude that seemed to have no place for the average worker and the greater good of the community.

"What I am saying is basically most of these corporations don't give a damn about whether the job is in the United States or abroad," LaFalce said in the committee's chambers, "and basically, the ones who are making the decisions feel no personal pain whatsoever. For that matter, they don't care that much about the pain they are causing to the individuals that are unemployed or to the communities that are adversely affected.

"Maybe they should have the right to make those painful decisions not painful to them, but painful to their former employees, painful to the communities where they used to live for twenty years, thirty years, fifty years, but it ought not to be the policy of the U.S. Government to promote that."9

Sweatshop Protests

But then figures like Santos began to get attention. Groups began to organize against "sweatshops," a term that had been used in the early 1900s to describe filthy, dark, and cramped factories where workers toiled all day and had few rights.

In May 1996, Kathie Lee Gifford tearfully announced on her television show that her line of clothing, sold in

Wal-Mart, was manufactured by Honduran girls making less than thirty-one cents an hour.

Sweatshop activists also pointed to a factory in San Salvador, where workers made fifty-five cents an hour sewing khaki pants and cotton shirts for Gap, a clothing company that reported $877 million in profits in 2000. The workers worked eighteen-hour shifts in a stifling factory. Bathroom breaks had to be requested, and bosses would not hesitate to deny those workers who displeased them. The water was foul and polluted.

Paid such meager wages, the workers could barely support themselves. One worker at the factory, Abigail Martínez, told *New York Times* reporters that she shared a two-room house with her parents, a sister, two brothers, and a grandmother.

In 1995, Martínez and a few other workers held strikes to protest working conditions. When the workers seized control of the factory, security guards used their guns as clubs to beat them into submission.

The violence attracted the attention of antisweat-shop groups in the United States. In the resulting glare of publicity, J.C. Penney and Target canceled their contracts with the factory. Gap agreed to stay, but only if conditions were improved. In response, the factory owners built a cafeteria. Ventilation brought fresh air through the building, and the bathrooms were made available to workers whenever they needed them. Gap paid outside monitors $10,000 a year to ensure the factory owners did not abuse workers.

Still, in 2001, Martínez made only five cents more an hour—sixty cents—than she did before the strikes.[10]

"Workers are suffering," said John Sweeney, president of the AFL-CIO. "They are losing their jobs or they are being exploited, and it's about time that these leaders of Congress and industry hear the story of what working conditions are like, and that they are reminded that they have a role to play in terms of addressing the issues of workers."[11]

This is not just limited to the United States. Through most of the 1980s the United States lost thousands of manufacturing jobs to nimbler, cheaper importers, especially the Japanese. But after the Japanese stock market collapsed in the early 1990s, the Japanese experienced a similar pattern. Japanese jobs were shipped overseas to cheaper importers, especially in Southeast Asia.

The tradition in Japan was for lifetime employment. But by 2001 large Japanese companies were cutting jobs, and the unemployment rate crept above 5 percent, the first time since 1953. Three million Japanese were unemployed.

"The wave of globalization can't be stopped," a Japanese business newspaper reported. "The unraveling of the lifetime employment system can't be turned back."[12]

Don't Do It!

The increasing reports of squalid factory conditions ignited a backlash. Nike, which had spent millions making its Swoosh one of the biggest brands in the world, now found itself the biggest target.

Some sports commentators began aiming barbs at the shoemaker. "Where's the Outrage? Sports World Just Ignores It. Nike Workers' Plight Doesn't Play at Final 4," shouted a *Philadelphia Daily News* headline.

"As the Arizona and Kentucky basketball players lace up their high-tops for tonight's college championship, thousands of Asian workers will sweat through another 12-hour day making Nike sneakers and clothes for next to nothing," wrote a reporter in disgust.[13]

While a recent report from a U.S. labor group condemned Nike practices, no one at the Final Four seemed to care. "It was business as usual," wrote the reporter. "A Nike-led carnival interrupted by a couple of basketball games."

The backlash got worse. Air Jordans had become so valuable to the street culture of America's inner cities that teenagers were shooting other teenagers for their shoes. Nike came under severe criticism for using low-wage labor to produce sneakers at far less than $30 pair and then selling them to poor kids for more than $100.

Leo Johnson, a director of youth activities for a housing project in Bronx, New York, and his coworker, Mike Gitelson, a social worker, had seen enough. They were furious that Nike would sell its shoes to American teenagers but not provide jobs for their parents. They were angry that Nike reinforced stereotypes—the only way a black American could make it out of the inner city was through rap music or sports.

"You're being suckered if you pay $100 for a sneaker that costs $5 to make," Johnson told the kids. "If somebody did that to you on the block, you know where it's going."

The kids sent Nike letters, complaining that they had spent $100 for a pair of sneakers that cost $30 to make and asking if Nike would be so kind as to return them the $70 difference.

When Nike answered with a form letter, the kids angrily dug out their old pairs of Nike sneakers and brought them to a Nike superstore in Manhattan, New York. As national network camera crews recorded the scene, they dumped garbage bags full of old, worn Nikes onto the store sidewalk.

One thirteen-year-old boy stood before a television camera and said words that must have made Nike executives shudder.

"Nike, we made you," he said. "We can break you."[14]

Globalization Is Good for the Globe

The intensity of the protests, and their appearance during a period of prosperity in much of the world, surprised many. Soon, proglobalization individuals and groups rallied in defense.

"Far from being the greatest cause of poverty, globalization is the only feasible cure," declared a well-known newsmagazine.[1]

The Glory and Benefits of Free Trade

Newark, a metropolis within sight of New York City, is one of the busiest ports in the world. Every day, enormous cargo ships steam into New York City's harbor. They carry goods and fly flags from dozens of countries. Guided by small tugs, the ships are gently eased into a stop along miles of docks. Once the ship is secured, cranes more than 150 feet (46 m) tall reach over the ship and scoop up the containers that sit stacked on the deck like giant Lego bricks.

Shipping containers are piled high on cargo ships near the port of Newark, New Jersey. Goods that are sold in local stores are brought on ships like these to the United States from countries all over the world.

The containers are then loaded onto hundred-car trains or hooked up to tractor-trailer trucks. The trains pull away. The tractor-trailers roar onto the fourteen-lane-wide New Jersey Turnpike. Goods of all varieties—baseballs, shirts, stereos, bananas, silverware, Oriental rugs, medicine, books—flow into the nation. Within days, sometimes hours, American consumers can choose from the labors of the entire world.

It is not just the dazzling selection provided by trade that makes it appealing. Trade promotes competition among industries. An American shoe factory must compete against a shoe factory in Asia. They must deliver a higher-quality shoe for a lower price, or the factory will go out of business. Facing competition, both factories will strive to become better and more efficient. The shopper, walking among racks of shoes at the store, gets the benefit.

Because of trade and competition, prices for many goods, including computers and electronics, have dropped while the quality has gone up. But what happens when one competing factory goes out of business? Supporters of free trade say that the increased efficiency of free trade will open up new opportunities, increase wealth, and give the fired workers a much better chance of finding another job.

One of the boldest experiments in free trade occurred in 1994, when the North American Free Trade Agreement (NAFTA) was passed and signed into law by President Bill Clinton. The treaty eliminated almost all trade barriers between the United States, Canada, and Mexico. It was passed despite the bitter opposition of American trade unions. How could American workers who earn close to $10 an hour, they asked, compete with Mexicans who earn less than $1 an hour?

At the presidential debates in 1992, candidate Ross Perot predicted gloomily before millions of television viewers that NAFTA would cause a "giant sucking sound" as American jobs were lost to foreign competition.

Almost ten years later, supporters of the treaty point out in triumph that the American economy has grown tremendously in the years since the passage of the bill.

Journalists and lawmakers still refer to the phrase "giant sucking sound," but only as a joke. American unemployment rates had dropped, not increased, after NAFTA passed. American living standards had risen, and the country enjoyed an economic boom through most of the 1990s.

In a speech before the bill was passed, President Clinton told a group of students at American University in Washington, D.C., that open markets are "the truth of our age" and help everyone: "It spurs us to innovate. It forces us to compete; it connects us with new customers. It promotes global growth without which no rich country can hope to grow wealthy. It enables our producers, who are themselves consumers of services and raw materials, to prosper. And so I say to you in the face of all the pressures to do the reverse, we must compete, not retreat."[2]

The Fruits of Trade

An even more aggressive experiment in free trade is the European Union (EU). Europe, a patchwork of warring countries for centuries, decided to voluntarily come together. For the past fifty years, a group of European countries—centered around France and Germany—lowered their barriers to trade. In January 2001 they introduced a common currency, the euro.

Europe, aided by the United States, has enjoyed virtually fifty years of prosperity. Whether the common currency will work as well as Europe hopes is still unclear. However, several nearby countries, such as Turkey and Romania, are eager to join the EU.

In return for membership, the countries must agree to the EU's standards of trade. More important, the countries

must respect human rights and have a democratic government. Encouraged by the chance to join the EU, those governments are cleaning up corruption, establishing fair laws, and giving their citizens more say in how the government is run.

A similar effect has occurred in the Western Hemisphere. In April 2001, thirty-four nations in North and South America agreed to work toward a free trade hemisphere with 800 million people. They also pledged that the benefits of membership would not be extended to any nation that was not a democracy. Communist Cuba, where Fidel Castro has ruled for more than forty years, was not invited.[3]

This, say supporters, is another benefit of globalization—not just free trade, but freedom itself. They point out that countries throughout history have shut themselves off from free trade. Almost without exception, these countries are ruled by dictators who stifle not only their citizens' rights, but also their imaginations.

Without competition, industries devour hundreds of man-hours producing goods that would be thrown out in a free market. Without fresh ideas, discoveries, and new experiences brought by mixing with others, the society grows rigid and blighted.

The Soviet Union is an example of a country that refused to open up through most of the 1900s. Its people suffered for decades, forced to buy poor-quality goods and live in shoddy housing. Its intellectuals faced persecution.

A current example is North Korea. The journalist who gets a rare chance to observe the country reports empty streets, huge gray statues of the current leaders, and a population on the brink of starvation.

Many other countries, especially in Africa and the Arab world, are also cut off from the outside world. They suffer under poverty and governments that give them few rights. It is these countries that need globalization the most, say supporters. They need free trade to bolster their economies and the examples of other countries to inspire democracy, the rule of law, and stability. Transnational corporations, though vilified by antiglobalization protesters, actually help the standards of living in the countries they enter, say supporters.

"They have an interest in the preservation of countries other than their own native land, and they want every place that they trade to do well. It's just part of the appeal of the global economy."[4]

"Multinational corporations tend to pull the world together. . . . They're sometimes criticized that they know no flag. Well, if nationalism has been the basis of most international conflict the last hundred years or so, then maybe that's not all bad that they don't have any flag," said George McGovern, the 1972 Democratic candidate for president.

The Success of Globalization

To many, the argument over globalization is best answered by simply looking around. The wealthiest, the most dynamic nations, are those that have opened themselves up. The nations of eastern Asia have raised their living standards dramatically in the past fifty years by participating in globalization. The nations that have been left out—especially in Africa and the Middle East—are falling further and further behind.

For this reason, many supporters of globalization have blasted protesters, calling them naive and destructive.

"While the protesters were busy denouncing globalization in the name of the world's poor," wrote a newspaper columnist, "[the world's poor] themselves will tell you that their problem with globalization is not that they are getting too much of it, but too little."

"By inhibiting global trade expansion they are choking the only route out of poverty for the world's poor. Which is why these 'protesters' should be called by their real name: The Coalition to Keep Poor People Poor."[5]

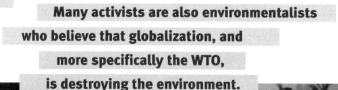

Many activists are also environmentalists who believe that globalization, and more specifically the WTO, is destroying the environment.

Killing the World to Save It?

Even if some believe that free trade does lead to more growth and prosperity—they argue that globalization is destroying the environment. Who, they ask, will be able to enjoy their wealth if the air is poisoned, the trees are cut down, and the water is polluted?

Activists blame corporations. Unconcerned with anything but growth, corporations use their power to get what they want. They demand raw materials—oil, timber, metals—and they don't care how many forests they cut or how much oil is spilled. It matters only that they make money and can report a profit at the end of the quarter.

To environmentalists, globalization and the environment are incompatible. Either globalization is stopped, or the world will be destroyed. The environmentalists have focused much of their rage on the WTO.

The WTO and the Environment

The WTO came into existence in 1995 as the successor to the GATT conferences. By the end of 2001, the WTO had

144 member countries. The purpose of the WTO, in broad terms, is to reduce trade barriers among nations.

When the WTO succeeded GATT, it also became stronger. Any of the member countries can be brought to court if trade agreements aren't met. The WTO is ruled by consensus. This means that a member can ignore a ruling from the WTO, but the pressure to conform is enormous.

To the fury and horror of activists, the WTO has used its influence to rule against many environmental and labor restrictions as illegal barriers to trade. Three examples are highlighted in *Whose Trade Organization?* printed by Public Citizen, a group that calls for the reform or abolition of the WTO.

In the 1990s, the U.S. Environmental Protection Agency (EPA) used the Clean Air Act to implement rules that would force oil companies to produce cleaner gasoline. Oil companies from Brazil and Venezuela, the latter of which is the largest exporter of gasoline to the United States, argued that the rules discriminated against them. The EPA, using complicated data to determine how much pollution was caused by gasoline, had implemented rules that could reject foreign gasoline as too dirty while allowing the same quality gasoline from U.S. producers.

The WTO decided in favor of Brazil and Venezuela, despite the United States' argument that the dirty gasoline would increase pollution. The United States, rather than face $150 million in tariffs on U.S. goods in Venezuela, agreed to lower the EPA's standards and allow dirtier gasoline to be sold. A troubling precedent had been set. Decisions made by Americans through their elected leaders had been overturned.[1]

The "Dolphin Death Act"

In 1972, Congress passed the Marine Mammal Protection Act. The act was amended in the 1980s to ban the sale of tuna captured with encirclement nets. The encirclement nets, dragged by fishing trawlers mostly in the eastern Pacific Ocean, scooped up tuna that were later processed and sold in supermarkets. But dolphins, who relish tuna, were also entangled and snarled in the nets. Millions of them drowned, and the nets were blamed for serious drops in dolphin species populations. Support to protect the dolphins was widespread. When legislation was passed, environmentalists said it reduced the number of annual deaths of dolphins from 100,000 to about 3,000.

But many foreign companies objected, calling the act protectionist. In 1990 challenges were made against the act in GATT, and both times GATT panels sided with the challengers. But because of GATT restrictions, the rulings against the Marine Mammal Protection Act were not enforced.

That was just as well to U.S. politicians, who didn't want to be seen publicly scrapping a law that was so popular. But President Clinton was under pressure from trade partners to end the ban on encirclement nets. In 1997 he supported a new bill. Supporters of the bill claimed that it would create a new global coalition to fight the slaughter of dolphins.

But environmentalists called it a cover to repeal the ban on encirclement nets. "It's the Dophin Death Act," said David Phillips, director of marine mammal studies at the Earth Island Institute, who helped lobby for the Marine Mammal Protection Act in the 1980s. Critics of the bill said the United States was capitulating to Mexico, a valuable trading partner, which operates several tuna fleets in the Pacific Ocean.

Representative George Miller (a Democrat from California), during debate on the bill, said it had nothing to do with protecting marine animals as its supporters claimed. "We are here because of international trade," he said.[2]

A compromise law, called the "International Conservation Dolphin Program Act," was passed. Though it contained some passages to protect dolphins, it did weaken the power of the U.S. government to restrict tuna caught in foreign encirclement nets.

Another terrible precedent was set, said environmentalists. GATT and WTO would always favor corporate, industrial interests over environmental and social regulations—deeming them barriers to trade.

The Sea Turtles

The next animal rights cause to fall to a WTO ruling was sea turtles. Congress passed a law in 1989 that required shrimp vessels to use special nets. Like the dolphins, sea turtles, many of them endangered species, were being caught in shrimp nets and drowned. The shrimpers were required to use nets with turtle excluder devices (or TEDs) that would allow turtles to slip out of the net through a trapdoor at the bottom.

Once again, foreign nations called the U.S. law an unfair penalty on their shrimp industry because they would have to outfit their ships with new nets. The WTO ruled in the shrimpers' favor, calling the U.S. law a deliberate attempt to block trade.

Environmentalists were enraged. "Why should we let a bunch of World Trade Organization bureaucrats determine the fate or our Earth?" said members of the Sea Turtles Restoration Project, an environmentalist group. Since then, the question has been repeated millions of times.

"You are talking about some animals that are on the brink of extinction, and the technology to save them is in the hundreds of dollars," David Schorr, director of sustainable commerce programs for the World Wildlife Fund, told a *Washington Post* reporter. "Yet the WTO so clearly says trade comes first."

Most infuriating to environmentalists and activists, however, was that the debate over the turtles was conducted in complete secrecy. No members of the media or

Sea turtles have been a focus of activists because the endangered animals become caught in shrimp nets and can drown.

public were allowed to be present at the WTO hearings, and no schedule was publicized.

Global Warming

Global warming has long alarmed environmentalists and, more recently, voters. While the rest of the world negotiated the Kyoto Treaty to limit greenhouse gas emissions, the United States under President George W. Bush pulled out and stood on the sideline, infuriating activists around the globe. In the United States it is still considered a fair argument to suggest that global warming is exaggerated, or perhaps not happening at all.

Since the Industrial Revolution, humankind has been burning oil, gas, coal, and wood at ever-increasing rates and, hence, producing carbon dioxide. Carbon dioxide has been piling up in the atmosphere, and carbon dioxide traps heat.

American politicians can resist this idea and the changes necessary to stop it, but global warming is being taken seriously by those who have an ulterior motive to take it seriously—the insurance industry.

The polar ice caps and glaciers are melting; the sea is rising. More heat has drawn more moisture into the air, causing more storms. Normally, no one would care about a few more summer showers or winter snowflakes. But these storms are huge—hurricanes with winds and water capable of wiping out whole cities. Insurance companies paid out $16 billion in storm-related claims through the 1980s. From 1990 to 1994, they had already paid out $48 billion.3

Carbon dioxide is not pollution. In the United States much of the air is in fact cleaner than it was ten years ago, but as more and more people burn more and more fossil fuels, more and more carbon dioxide is released into the atmosphere. This spreads around the world, which means the world is heating up and will continue to heat up.

As more of the world is developed, more fossil fuels will be burned as forests are cleared and factories are built. As living standards rise, more people will want the benefits of middle-class society—refrigerators, lights, heat in the winter, air-conditioning in the summer, SUVs. Fossil fuel consumption will rise even more.

The development championed by the IMF and the World Bank appears on a collision course with nature as we know it. Transnational corporations tend to downplay environmental concerns, because rules to save nature smack of government intervention and costly regulations.

President George W. Bush has been called the "toxic Texan" because he would not sign the Kyoto Treaty, which required the United States to limit its emissions of greenhouse gases. His own plan to reduce pollution was dubbed "hot air" by the *Economist*.

In March 2002 an iceberg the size of Rhode Island broke away from Antarctica. Scientists were stunned by the size of the berg, saying it was the first time in thousands of years that the continent had seen so much ice erode so quickly. Many in the scientific community were not quick to blame global warming, but they could offer no other explanation.

"With the disappearance of ice shelves that have existed for thousands of years, you rather rapidly run out of other explanations," said Dr. Theodore A. Scambos, a glaciologist at the National Snow and Ice Data Center at the University of Colorado.[4]

Activists wonder aloud how many corporate head-quarters will be submerged when coastal cities around the world are flooded.

Globalization Will Save the Globe

Critics contend that the environmentalists' view of the perfect world—trees, mountains, untouched meadows, pristine oceans—rarely has a human being in it. The environmentalists, say critics, treat people as if they were a disease or a problem to be solved.

This attitude has led to the passage of thousands of laws and books filled with regulations that dictate how people and industry can treat the environment. This has had some remarkable success, but it doesn't answer the needs pressing the environment today. Laws, regulations, and pollution controls stifle creativity, say critics, and can cost millions in time spent in court.

Instead, they say, unleash industry to solve the problem. Industry and the free market are the sources of some of history's greatest ideas. They have pushed up the production of dairy cows, made computers the size of your hand, and put men on the Moon.

These are miracles that can be put to the service of the environment, say supporters. The biggest free market today is the world itself. The solution to the globe's environmental troubles is more globalization.

Supporters of globalization and the free market have argued that globalization rewards technological innovation—innovation that will lead to a cleaner world. Globalization will also bring prosperity, and with prosperity people can turn to cleaning up their environment.

As poor countries industrialize, they rely on coal as the cheapest form of available energy. Environmentalists are worried that China will evolve into a huge, dirty consumer society that will pollute the entire world. Many towns in China are already dominated by smokestacks and factories.

Supporters of globalization see evidence in the industrial regions of Europe and North America. Fifty years ago, those areas were massively polluted. The cities of northern Great Britain were darkened by soot burned from coal. In the United States near Cleveland, a river was so filthy that the layer of debris and chemicals on its surface caught fire. Observers remarked that they had never seen a river burn before.

Today, however, North America and Europe are among the cleanest areas on Earth, even while still enjoying a high standard of living. The question is whether other countries can develop without going through the environmental upheaval the industrialized nations experienced.

President Bush has proposed using a system of credits for industries to allow them a certain number of pollutants. The plan intends to encourage industries to use their money, technology, and know-how to create solutions to environmental problems.

In Europe, governments use "green taxes" against industries and practices that pollute the environment. They calculate the amount of tax that's necessary to compensate for the cost of pollution.

When being environmental makes good business sense, then the world will have a true environmental revolution, say supporters. But because industry has rarely ever undertaken environmental measures unless forced, environmentalists remain skeptical.

Whose Culture?

In August 1999 a French farmer named Jose Bove led a group armed with crowbars, wrenches, and sledgehammers into a McDonald's construction site in Millau, a town in southern France. The group swarmed over the unfinished fast-food restaurant, smashing equipment, glass, and just about everything else. Bove was caught by police and sent to jail for twenty days. When he was released, he was greeted as a hero.

Bove's act struck a chord. To many, McDonald's represents the face of globalization, which sweeps away local cultures and enforces a bland conformity. Bove accused McDonald's of promoting destructive farming that wiped out smaller farmers. This was not an act against the United States, Bove told reporters, but an act of a small farmer against an impersonal, global corporation. Bove noted that American farmers had contributed $5,000 for his bail money. "There are more similarities than differences between us," he said. "We are fighting for the same things."[1]

Jose Bove emerges from court a hero to many antiglobalization activists who believe McDonald's represents the essence of globalization.

Globalization Is Americanization

After the collapse of the Soviet Union, the United States straddled the globe as the undisputed world power. Its economy was the largest, its military the most powerful, its culture dominant. But along with this power has come unprecedented attention and resentment.

For many people in the world, globalization and Americanization are the same. They see an advancing tide of American youth culture—fast-food franchises, rap music, MTV, and *Star Wars* movies.

This makes many people nervous. To some, the United States is forcing its ideals, its economic structure, even its culture and language on the rest of the world. They call it "cultural imperialism."

"Never before in modern history has a country dominated the earth so totally as the United States does today," wrote the German magazine *Der Spiegel* in 1997. "The Americans are acting, in the absence of limits put to them by anybody and anything, as if they own a blank check in their 'McWorld.'"[2]

By the 1990s, American "soft power" seemed virtually unstoppable. In Spain, Great Britain, Germany, and Italy, at least nine of the top-ten movies in 1998 came from the United States. McDonald's restaurants, of which there are more than 29,000 franchises in 121 countries, feed 1 percent of the world's population every day.

At antiglobalization protests, the most common targets are franchises of American companies—such as Starbucks and McDonald's. Anti-Americanism, which varies in intensity and degree according to its location, is growing.

The "Angry Man Syndrome"

The angriest are those who rage that globalization is leaving them out or leaving them behind. *New York Times* columnist Thomas Friedman described these people as afflicted with "angry man syndrome."

Friedman paraphrased a conversation he had with historian Ronald Steel to explain the phenomenon. Steel described how Americanization-globalization seems unstoppable. It's on your television. If you turn off television, it's on your cell phone. If you throw out your phone, it's on the Internet. If you destroy all electronics in your home, it's outside on a billboard or a KFC franchise in your neighborhood.

"And it's not only in the room with you, this Americanization-globalization. You eat it. It gets inside you. And when it comes in it often blows open a huge gap between fathers and sons, mothers and daughters, grandparents and grandchildren. It creates a situation where one generation sees the world radically different from their parents, and it's all America's fault."[3]

Globalizing the World, America Is Globalized

But many argue that this perception is not only exaggerated, it's simply wrong. America's cultural strength has influenced many cultures, but it has never been a one-way process.

The United States, a nation of immigrants, still attracts talented and ambitious people from all over the world. It has also been influenced by the styles of dress, customs, and food the immigrants have brought with them.

Any American city today has McDonald's and Burger King, but it will also likely have a dozen Greek diners, Chinese takeouts, sushi bars, and Indian restaurants.

American sports are dominated by non-Americans. Baseball players such as Sammy Sosa, Roberto Alomar, and Pedro Martinez come from Latin America. The NBA has been flooded with European stars. In the 2002 season, fifty-two players from thirty-one countries played in the league. "The young guys, especially from Europe, are basically saying: 'OK, this is America. We can take this over.'" Buoyed by the contribution of teammates Peja Stojakovic and Hedo Turkoglu, Sacramento forward Chris Webber said during the 2002 playoffs, "I love that attitude."4

Only three NBA teams finished the 2002 season without a foreign player on their roster, and they finished their seasons early. Not one made the playoffs. But perhaps the greatest sign of America's reception to globalization can be found in its most common and identifiable product—Hollywood. By 2001 more than half of the people who paid to watch Hollywood movies lived outside the United States.

At the Oscars in March 2001, a movie in Chinese—*Crouching Tiger Hidden Dragon*—was nominated for Best Picture, one of three foreign films to receive such an honor in the academy's seventy-three-year history.

"This is a great cultural phenomenon. That's great encouragement, of course, for the folks at home and Chinese filmmakers," said director Ang Lee. "But I think it's a great cultural event here as well."

Almost half of the actors and actresses nominated for awards lived outside the United States. They included Russell Crowe from Australia, Juliette Binoche from France, and Judi Dench from the United Kingdom. A CNN headline effectively summed it up, "More than Ever, Oscars Go Global."

The same trend can be found in music, where an explosion of recordings and distribution on the Internet has exposed audiences to "world music." World music pulls from separate traditions and is influenced by everything available—the chants of monks, African and South American rhythms, guitar music of the American South.

Many artists find globalization a source of extraordinary inspiration. They dismiss arguments from those who say cultures must be preserved.

"Which cultures have ever remained identical and unchanged over time?" asked the Peruvian writer Mario Vargas Llosa. "To find them, we must search among the small and primitive magical-religious communities that live in caves, worship thunder and beasts, and, due to their primitivism, are increasingly vulnerable to exploitation and extermination.

"All other cultures, in particular those that have the right to be called modern and alive, have evolved to the point that they are but a remote reflection of what they were just two or three generations before."[5]

Protest

The antiglobalization cause has attracted thousands of groups. Commentators and journalists have remarked that almost anyone enraged at anything can blame it on globalization.

An antiglobalization rally is a blend and mishmash of groups and people who seem to have little in common. They can be feminists lobbying for more freedom for women; union workers who want to save their jobs; anarchists who hate all political organization; environmental groups who hope to save the whales; activists protesting racism. They are students and seniors; hopeful and bitter; peaceful and violent.

And whenever there is a global meeting, you can be sure they'll be there.

At the G-8 meeting in Genoa, Italy, in July 2001, protesters lit bonfires and were chased down by baton-wielding police on horseback. At the World Economic Forum in New York City in February 2002, they filled the sidewalks outside a flagship Gap store on Fifth Avenue and yelled at the windows while shoppers nervously examined sale items.

During the G-8 protests in Italy on July 19, 2001, a group of Iranians conduct mock hangings as they demand a boycott of the industrialized nations' increasing business in Iran.

When Bush flew to New York City on July 9, 2002, to give an hour-long speech on corruption, they were there, packed into a corner behind police barricades on Wall Street. "Two-Four-Six-Eight! We want Bush to regulate!" they chanted, as the presidential car whizzed by.

Not everyone approves of these tactics. Naomi Klein, author of the antiglobalization book *No Logo,* criticized the protesters as "meeting stalkers, following the trade bureaucrats as if they were the Grateful Dead."

Despite the criticism that has been directed at protesters in the past years, the antiglobalization movement can claim successes. It is one of the genuine movements

Opponents of the World Economic Forum in New York City on February 2, 2002, carry signs protesting the involvement of top U.S. leaders Secretary of Defense Donald Rumsfeld, President George W. Bush, and Vice President Dick Cheney.

of our time, a passionate and growing voice in world issues today. That voice is not always easily understandable, since antiglobalization groups vary so greatly. Some are chaotic. Others are well financed and organized.

Global Exchange, based in San Francisco, has a budget of $4 million and a staff of several dozen. Fifty Years Is Enough is a U.S.-based organization that lobbies against the World Bank and the IMF and is run by Njoki Njoroge Njehu, a Kenyan. Ralph Nader, the activist and occasional presidential candidate, founded Public Citizen, an organization dedicated to fighting a list of abuses. Students Against Sweatshops has chapters in campuses all over the country.

These groups do not share the same message or agree on protest tactics. Some believe in peaceful protest, others insist that only destruction of property and confrontation with police will spread their message. Still others disagree that demonstrations do anything constructive at all. Some activists prefer to take their message directly to people, by speaking to groups, selling books, and distributing pamphlets.

An Activist

In October 2001, a tall, bald fifty-one-year-old man walked to the front of a crowded auditorium at Hofstra University, New York.

"We should abolish the IMF and the World Bank," he announced in a booming voice. "It sounds strong, but we abolished slavery, Jim Crow, the 60-hour work week. 'Abolish' is a good word."

Meet Kevin Danaher, an activist who has been speaking at college campuses about social issues and globalization for the past twenty-five years. "The corporations have taken over the government and the public airwaves," he continued. "Who runs the department of transportation? The auto companies that they are supposed to watch."

His voice grew angrier and louder. "Jesus only whipped one group—the bankers," he said. "Who runs the world? The bankers."

His audience laughed.

"And I'm not trashing rich people," he added. "I love rich people." But the values of the past five hundred years, money and violence, he said, have to be replaced with values that are more in tune with the natural cycles of the environment.

"I criticize this country because I love it. I've hitchhiked across it and been to every state," Danaher said. "I love the people of this country. Great people. Bad government. It's like that everywhere."

Danaher has made a similar speech at many university campuses, to student groups large and small. The night before, he had given a talk at the University of Massachusetts. The next day, he would speak in New Jersey.

Danaher received the most applause of the six panelists speaking that day. After his talk, a group of people crowded around Danaher, who pulled out several books on globalization and offered them for sale. There were many takers.

"I really liked what you said," said a college student dressed in a dark jean jacket.

"I have never been so inspired," said a man in his fifties. Danaher thanked them both. After the crowd diminished, Danaher put his suitcases on a pull cart and walked out of the auditorium, ready to move on to his next engagement.

Danaher is one of many speakers who crisscross the country every year to speak to students and civic groups about globalization and the harm they say it is causing our world. The overwhelming mood among the students, he said, is cynicism.

"And cynicism is a word for insight when courage is lacking," he said, a phrase he has obviously repeated many times before. "We have to change the conditions that have caused so many people to get frustrated. We need a global grass roots movement to counter this global capitalist movement—and it's happening."

But he sees a lot of frustration. "A lot of people are stuck in the angry phase," he said. "People know the system sucks. Plenty of people are critical of global poverty but what do they do about it?"[1]

Why Abolish the IMF and the World Bank?

One thing they can do, said Danaher, is support groups and policies that abolish the IMF and the World Bank. The core problem with the two institutions is that they support and perpetuate a system that is not only based on inequality, but increases it, say antiglobalization activists.

To see that inequality, they say, take a look at two societies that largely champion globalization: the United States and the United Kingdom. They point out that in the 1980s, Margaret Thatcher in the United Kingdom and

Ronald Reagan in the United States introduced reforms into their economies that favored business and sharply increased inequality.

Over the past twenty years in the United States, the rich have gotten richer and the poor have gotten poorer, according to The Milken Institute, a group that studies the world economy, and New York University economist Edward N. Wolff. Using Federal Reserve data from the period between 1983 and 1998, Wolff showed that the number of households worth more than $1 million doubled to 4.78 million. Those worth $10 million quadrupled to 239,000.

But, as Ted Redburn of *The New York Times* noted, "That's great. A rich society like the United States should have plenty of rich people—and the more the merrier. But what is disturbing is what happened to just about everybody else."

Of the growth in wealth, a meager 9 percent went to the bottom 80 percent of the U.S. population. Or, the top 20 percent of the population received 91 percent of the growth.

"The results indicate rather dramatically," wrote Wolff, "that the fruits from economic growth in the last few decades were enjoyed by a surprisingly small part of the population—the top 20 percent, and particularly the richest 1 percent."[2]

Charles Kernaghan, director of the National Labor Committee, has drawn even more stark contrasts. He calculated that a Haitian worker laboring to sew apparel for Disney would have to work more than sixteen years (at eighteen cents an hour) to make what CEO executive Michael Eisner makes in one hour—$9,783.[3] When Eisner was confronted in 1997 by angry stockholders about his $400 million multiyear pay, he was unimpressed.

"I don't think people understand executive compensation," he said.[4]

Most people don't, and the antiglobalization forces have wondered why anyone would support an economic system that gives a laborer 18 cents an hour and the boss almost $10,000.

Eisner is not an exception. Executive pay rose from 42 times that of the average worker in 1980 to 475 times it in 1999.[5]

Conservatives, such as radio talk show host Rush Limbaugh, say that the free market mobilizes the potential of society. The individual, working for his or her own self-interest, is driven to ever-higher levels of achievement. These achievements bring medical breakthroughs, new technology, more employment, and wealth. Everyone benefits. The market will find the solution to mankind's ills.

But critics of free market capitalism call self-interest by a less flattering word—greed. How can people chasing their own greed help society? asked economist John Maynard Keynes. Capitalism is driven only by the desire for more wealth, say protesters, and consequently brushes aside the things that make life worth living—culture, nature, community.

Even the way we measure progress and growth, say protesters, is skewed.

"For example, let's say I go into a bar and drink ten beers. All the money I spent on that beer is a positive contribution to the GNP," writes Kevin Danaher in *10 Reasons to Abolish the IMF & World Bank.* "Now I'm drunk. I drive away in my car, and I crash into a family in their car.

They're all maimed, and require intensive medical care for the rest of their lives. The tow truck, the emergency crews, the court costs, any jail time I get sentenced to, and the lifetime of medical care for the victims are all positive additions to GNP."[6]

A similar skewed perception of progress has marred the suburbs of the United States. For the last four decades, Americans have been moving out of crowded cities to enjoy the nature and serenity of the suburbs. Local town councils encouraged housing developments and businesses.

And what happened? Today, suburbanites face traffic congestion, pollution, and ugly strip malls. A trip to the grocery store has become a half-hour battle with other motorists broken by long pauses at traffic lights. Suburbanites are now asking themselves what the point of "growth" is if it makes a place unlivable.

Opponents of development came up with a name for this kind of growth—sprawl. In the northeastern United States, sprawl has become so severe that town councils are desperately buying open space and farms before they are developed and lost forever. Most of those efforts are too late.

The question of the environment is now hitting home among Americans. What's the point of having money in my pocket if I can't drink the water or breathe the air because it's too polluted?

The connection between congested New Jersey suburbs and the policies of the World Bank may not be obvious, but they both come out of a common perception of what economic prosperity means. The IMF and the World Bank promote one vision; many antiglobalization protesters are advocating another.

To Danaher, this fits in with his view of the world—"great people, bad government."

Using a pen, Danaher draws two triangles side by side on a piece of paper. He colors in the top of each triangle. "These are the elites in each nation," he explains. "They only talk to each other."

He points to the uncolored parts of the triangle. "Our goal is to disrupt the communication between the elites and make it a grassroots communication." Grassroots communication, he believes, empowers people and fosters democracy, and a true democracy can regulate globalization properly so all people are protected.

Danaher reminds the listener that he's not against globalization itself, he's against a globalization without rules.[7]

Globalization, Money, and Democracy

Globalization corrupts democracy, say activists. Drawing on their billions of dollars, corporations can buy leaders and global institutions. Global activists want to build a wall between wealth and power.

"Globalization requires the undermining of democracy at home," said Danaher. "We get cheap sneakers, but there's a price."

In the United States, money has become an integral part of government. After Congress passed bills that would hand $25 billion to corporations, economist and *New York Times* columnist Paul Krugman wrote in disgust, "Cynics tell us that money has completely corrupted our politics, that in the last election big corporations basically bought themselves a government that will serve their interests.

Several related events last week suggest that the cynics have a point."[8]

The influence of wealth, so evident in the U.S. government, is even more extreme in the institutions of world government, where they operate behind closed doors.

"Why We Protest"

Those closed doors are a very sore point to protesters. In an editorial written for the *Washington Post*, Robert Weissman, codirector of the Washington-based organization Essential Action, presented four demands to the IMF and the World Bank.

The first was to open IMF and World Bank sessions to the public and media. Weissman noted that the details of loans are not released until after they have been approved, effectively cutting out any debate or public participation in the decision.

"The U.S. Congress operates in light of day; federal regulations are proposed for public comment before adoption. Why shouldn't similar sunlight shine on the IMF and World Bank?" asked Weissman.

The second demand was to relieve the crushing debts held by countries in the Third World. Many poor countries, said Weissman, must spend more money servicing debt than on hospitals or schools.

The third was to end the demands that the loan recipient's budget be balanced. This policy often guts social, health, and educational programs. One example, wrote Weissman, was the introduction of fees at a Nairobi health clinic, which "led to a decline in attendance of 40 percent for men and nearly two-thirds for women."

Weissman also railed against the privatization of essential services, such as clean water, "despite evidence that privatization leads to higher charges, decreased access for the poor to clean water and the spread of disease."

Last, he claimed the World Bank has to stop lending money for projects that despoil the environment and local societies. Weissman pointed out that the IMF and the World Bank have had a poor track record, especially when considering that Latin America has had stagnant growth and Africa has slid even deeper into poverty.

"The only developing countries that have done well in that time are Asian countries that largely ignored the standard prescriptions of the IMF and World Bank," he wrote.

"Another world is possible. If the IMF and World Bank operated transparently, if poor countries were relieved from the straitjacket of debt, if the institutions did not impose user fees for health care and other harmful policies, then countries would be much freer to pursue different economic strategies in accordance with the democratic determinations of their people. We share these modest democratic aspirations with people across the globe."[9]

One Solution

When asked, most activists agree that globalization is inevitable. They simply want it to be fairer, with more wealth shared with the workers.

Bryan Hirsch, a student at the University of Pennsylvania, has a favorite quote, which he attributes to Albert Einstein. "The world is a dangerous place to live" he says, "not because of the people who are evil, but because of the people who don't do anything about it." The quote is the basis of Hirsch's approach to his life, and he is determined not to let globalization just happen.

Raised in a community outside San Francisco, California, Hirsch was conscious of social and environmental issues. By the time he was five, he stopped eating red meat. As a teenager, he summered in the Rocky Mountains at a camp that offered vegan meals. He soon resolved to become an activist.

"When I came to the University of Pennsylvania," he says, "I thought environmental issues [were] going to be my thing." The protests in Seattle, he says, "got the wheels turning." In 2000 he became conscious of labor issues and joined the university's Students Against Sweatshops group. Hirsch took part in the group's protests against university apparel manufactured in low-wage factories.

While spending a summer in Ecuador, Hirsch learned of a village where families used handlooms to weave clothing. Hirsch decided to take the clothes woven by the villagers—bags, scarves, gloves, hats, sweaters—and sell them at Penn.

At a Christmas sale, he made $8,000, which he sent back to the families. At another sale, he made $17,000. The money was sent back to the village, where it makes a difference in the lives of the villagers. It is a link, he said, that allows workers to benefit directly from their labor.

It is a small start, which Hirsch says he hopes will grow in size and stature. Possibly, he says, it will become a model of prosperity that is not limited to just those on top.[10]

chapter eight

The IMF Faces a Meltdown

Economic Crisis in Mexico and Asia

By the mid-1990s the world had come closer together than it ever had in history. This was demonstrated during 1997 and 1998, a period of sudden economic turmoil. In hindsight, it was a fascinating year, a time when an observer could literally watch the world economy break apart and the IMF desperately try to put it back together again. Not only did world leaders come to grips with how integrated the world had become, but they also confronted the fact that the policies of the organizations of globalization—the IMF especially—needed drastic reform.

The "Tequila Crisis"

The first hint of trouble appeared in Mexico.

In the mid-1980s, Mexican reformers, many of them educated in universities in the United States, proposed changing the structure of the Mexican economy. Taxes and regulations protected Mexican industry from foreign competition. The reformers wanted this to end, which it did, and by the late 1980s, the Mexican president was proposing that Mexico join a free trade agreement with the United States and Canada.

Through the early 1990s the Mexican economy enjoyed another boom. Investor money flowed into the country, building factories, supplying jobs, and giving workers higher wages. The nation's wealth increased, while inflation stayed low.

What became known as the Tequila Crisis began in 1994, when the Mexican government decided to devalue its currency, the peso. They hoped a cheaper currency would make Mexican goods easier to sell in the world, thus leading to more orders and spurring growth. But when speculators heard that the peso was falling, they sold even more than the government expected. The price of the peso crashed far lower than the government intended. The result was financial panic. Investors pulled their money out of the country because the peso was worth far less than it had been before. At the same time, the Mexican government now had to exchange far more pesos to pay the money it owed foreigners.

The Mexican economy shrank by a devastating 7 percent. Workers were laid off and businesses failed. To stabilize the Mexican economy, the United States provided a $50 billion loan. The stopgap measure worked. After two years, investor panic had waned and growth had resumed.

But, as Paul Krugman wrote in *The Return of Depression Economics,* it seems the true lessons of the Tequila Crisis were never learned. The financial crisis, first of all, seemed out of proportion to Mexico's mistake, which was simply a botched currency devaluation.

Something appeared to be fundamentally wrong with the system, but few in the 1990s were prepared to look hard at the problem.

The other mistake was the confidence generated by the success of the bailout. If another economy had a similar panic, investors reasoned, the economists and government leaders would make sure everything turned out all right.

But that's not what happened when the next string of crises occurred.[1]

Asia Rising

They were called the "Asian Tigers"—Indonesia, Malaysia, Thailand, and the Philippines. While the rest of the world economies grew moderately, the Asian Tigers roared. Rarely before in history, a well-known economist noted, had economies grown so much so fast.

The growth attracted investors, who lined up to extend a seemingly endless stream of credit. The boom continued. Japan and the United States relocated many of their factories to Southeast Asia, and orders for goods poured in from around the world.

The goods went out and the cash flowed in. The incomes of Southeast Asians rose steadily, and a middle class appeared that reveled in consumption. Eager shoppers flooded shiny new malls, packing shopping carts full of items such as coats, cosmetics, VCRs, and microwave ovens. To explain the Southeast Asian success, some commentators said the people possessed "Asian values"—a unique combination of diligence, thrift, and patience.

The Asian Tigers

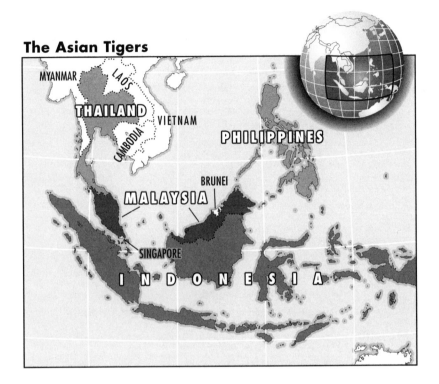

But in 1997, the Asian Tigers were struck by an economic hurricane that brought the global economic system to the brink of collapse. A few terrifying months showed how advanced globalization had become.

The Currency Speculators

The problem started in early 1997, when currency speculators began selling Asian currencies.

Who and what are currency speculators? They are a product of globalization. Using high-speed computers, currency speculators around the world monitor global economies. With one press of the button, they can transfer billions of dollars of money from one country to the next, leaving behind crippled economies and chaos.

Jack Weatherford, in his book *The History of Money*, described currency speculators as a new immense power, a bunch of financial wizards who dwarf banks, corporations, and governments.

> At any second of the day, thousands of traders stand poised to react, and even more computers stand ready to buy and sell as soon as the numbers line up in the statistically programmed pattern. The many virtually simultaneous decisions of people throughout the world create a large supply of electronic money that moves like a carefully trained and choreographed flock of birds that take flight in a moment, all headed in the same direction and able to change course in midstream. This currency flock roams the earth by night and day, alighting here and there before taking off for another pond or field on the other side of the world.[2]

In effect, currency speculators judge a country as if it were a company. They examine the country's economic policies, its budget, whether its regulations are friendly to business or not, and whether it has a large trade deficit. If the country's economy is sound and strong, the speculators can buy billions of dollars' worth of the economy's money, driving up its price. They later sell it for a profit. But if the speculators suspect that the country's economy is weakening, the process is reversed. They may initiate a selling frenzy that can cause a currency to crash.

In such cases, the country's central bank can defend its currency by raising interest rates, thus making it more attractive to investors. The investors buy the currency and keep the price stable.

But raising interest rates also makes it more difficult to do business in a country. For one thing, it's more expensive to take out loans. Without loans, homes aren't bought and factories aren't built. Economic growth is choked, leaving jobless workers protesting in the streets.

So governments are put in a tough position. They need to keep the value of the currency up, but they also don't want to force their own economy to go into a painful recession.

Governments have another option. They can buy the money as the speculators sell it, thus propping up its value. But this requires the central bank to have a large store of money reserves to keep pace. Often, the central bank runs out of money, forcing it to "devalue" the currency, or watch helplessly as it tumbles on its own.

When this happens, the country's economy and pride are dealt a humiliating blow before the entire world, and the economy is often left in shambles.

A falling currency can destabilize an entire region. If Thailand's currency falls, its neighbors are put in a difficult position. T-shirts, televisions, and computers made in Thailand are now less expensive than those made in, say, the Philippines. Suddenly, factories in the Philippines are closing because no one is buying their products anymore. The Philippine currency is the next to fall. The result is a domino effect.

Far more important, investors lose confidence and pull their money out of the economy. Why? If an investor lends a Thailand company $1 million, he must convert the dollars into Thai currency to buy stock. But if the Thai currency begins to fall in value, the $1 million will fall with it. If the Thai currency falls 25 percent, the $1 million will be worth only $750,000. And that's before it has even been spent. Investors will pull their money out of Thailand as soon as possible.

Without foreign investors demanding to buy stocks on the Thai market, the price of stocks collapses. When companies can't raise money on the stock market, companies cannot pay back their debts. When companies lose the ability to pay their debts, the banks that lent them money fail and close their doors. Investment dries up, growth shrinks, workers are laid off, prices rise. Hence, falls in currency can trigger an economic meltdown.

No country, not even the largest and most stable, is immune to the speculations of currency traders. Not surprisingly, government leaders and bureaucrats around the globe hate currency traders.

In June 1995, Jacques Chirac, the president of France, called speculators the "AIDS of our economies."[3]

The Asian Crisis

But why did the disease hit the Asian economies? It had become increasingly clear that the red-hot Asian economies were not following the rules of the free market. Theoretically, the free market is ruthless but efficient. It directs capital into investments that demand returns. But in the Asian economies, dictators gave family members and friends great power in directing where the money was spent and how. Observers dubbed it "crony capitalism."

In Malaysia, seventy-two-year-old Premier Mahathir bin Mohamad wanted a building taller than any other in the world. Using foreign investment dollars, he built the Petronas Towers, a 1,483-foot (452-m)-tall skyscraper that soars above the Kuala Lumpur skyline. Mohamad had a passion for tall things. Additional money was spent on the world's tallest flagpole and the world's tallest control tower. This was not capitalism, this was a waste of money, and it wasn't isolated to Malaysia.

In Indonesia, the direction of building projects—roads, factories, dams, bridges—ended up in the hands of relatives of President Suharto. Worse, officials had to be routinely bribed, further skimming off funds. When investors were willing to lend money, the easy access to funds led to poor investments. Hotels were built that no one needed. Golf courses were laid out before anyone considered who would play there.

While the Asian economies were steadily growing, these problems could be glossed over or ignored. But after 1995, Southeast Asian exports began to fall, and still the loans, the projects, the bribes had to be paid off. When returns fell, investors started to lose confidence, and then they began to pull out.

As investors traded the Indonesian money—called the baht—into dollars, the law of supply and demand swung viciously into effect. The supply of baht grew while demand for it fell. Consequently, the value of the baht began to slide. To counter the slide, the Thai government stepped in and began buying baht. They also raised interest rates, in effect saying they would pay more to investors to keep their money in Thai banks as baht.

By July, however, the Thai government had run out of money, and it announced that it would no longer intervene to keep the baht's value high. On July 2, the Thai currency fell 12 percent against the dollar. By the end of 1997, the baht was worth half of what it was worth in July.

The first domino of what would become a worldwide economic crisis had fallen. Stock markets in Southeast Asia crashed 35 percent, dragging down real-estate prices. Banks that had invested in real estate were ruined. Because the currencies had fallen, foreign loans had suddenly ballooned.

And it wasn't just limited to the East Asian economies. The world was smaller than it had ever been, and an economic crisis in one country produced shockwaves that roiled the world economic market. In New York City, investors feared that American companies would be hurt by falling sales in Asia. The stock market fell more than two hundred points in two days.

In just one year, the Asian Tiger economies were left shattered. The central banks of each country were forced to raise interest rates, stifling economic growth. Country budgets were slashed, deficits swelled, and the easy flow of foreign money abruptly went dry.

The economic fall was sudden and shocking, and the shockwaves threatened to disrupt the stability of entire societies. In Indonesia, President Suharto, who had ruled Indonesia for thirty-two years, seemed unable to comprehend what had happened. Per capita income for the nation of 200 million plunged from $1,200 to $300. Wealth evaporated, corporations were left unable to pay back more than $70 billion they owed investors. The proud towers of the business district in Jakarta were suddenly vacant.4

People were unable to pay for food, much less pay their bills. Angry crowds gathered in the streets of Jakarta to demand reform and an end to Suharto's leadership. When police units fired on the crowds and killed six students, the capital exploded in fury, riots, and looting.

A mob seized control of a toll road leading to the airport and demanded cash from anyone who passed through. Students, who had been agitating for democracy for months, grew increasingly bold. "Suharto must be thrown out like a dog," read graffiti outside a university.5

When the economy collapsed in Malaysia, Mohamad furiously blamed the outside world and what the currency speculators—especially billionaire George Soros. "All these countries have spent 40 years trying to build up their economies and a moron like Soros comes along," he complained.

Desperate, Mohamad begged rich Malaysians to go abroad, pawn off their jewelry, and return to deposit the money in the treasury. To stave off food bills, he urged citizens to plant vegetables in their front gardens. Most drastic, he ended the sale of the Malaysian currency to speculators, effectively withdrawing from the world economy.

The disintegration of the Asian economies was frightening, but what followed was terrifying. The Asian crisis appeared to have unnerved investors around the globe. The crisis spread into Latin America and South America. Brazil saw $11 million pulled out of its economy in five weeks.

The IMF Bailout

Riding in to the rescue, the IMF stepped in with loan packages to save the economies. Thailand, the source of the crisis, was promised more than $17 billion. Another $23 billion was dispatched to Indonesia.

But everyone wondered if it was enough. Already the South Korean currency was falling in value. South Korea, however, was no economic lightweight. In the decades after the Korean War in the 1950s, the Korean people had built a strong, successful economy that was the eleventh largest in the world.

IMF director Michel Camdessus said the loans to Thailand and Indonesia would end the crisis and return stability to the region. Yes, he noted, the South Korean currency had been falling against the dollar, but "I don't believe that the situation in South Korea is as alarming as the one in Indonesia a couple of weeks ago."

But investors did. In November, the South Korean stock market plunged as jittery investors, worried that the falling currency would eat up profits, pulled out. Another domino had fallen.

The South Korean currency tumbled. Desperate for foreign cash, South Korean companies sold products, such as steel, at incredibly cheap prices. Now other industries around the world were placed under pressure.

Near panic ensued. The economies of eastern Asia had become a huge, smoking train wreck. If South Korea fell apart, then the contagion could spread to Japan—the world's second-largest economy. Japan was large and powerful but also crippled because of bad loans, slow growth, and weak political leadership. If Japan fell, then there was only one domino left before the entire global economy utterly collapsed—the United States.

The IMF was not about to let that happen. When a humiliated South Korea asked the IMF for help in November 1997, the IMF agreed. The next month, Camdessus pledged an astounding $57 billion in loans.

"Tough Love"

The economic tsunami of 1997 showed a nasty, unpredictable side of globalization. The IMF's attempt to restore order showed another side—a vision of how the world could be run. It is this vision, described below, that attracts so many angry protesters to world economic meetings.

The IMF's loans are not charity. When a country agrees to the loans, they also agree to reform their economies according to a formula that is "tough love." There may be some pain for the societies to reform themselves and rid themselves of bad habits, reasoned the IMF leaders, but it would all be for the better in the long run.

The IMF's formula varies for each country—but it shares the same characteristics. Each country is ordered to focus less on growth and more on reforming the structure of its economy. Banks have to be reorganized, markets opened, all government and company financial dealings made available to investor scrutiny. Interest rates must be raised to steady inflation and restore the currency. Government budget deficits must be tamed.

After these measures are taken, said the IMF, the economy will grow and become strong, delivering prosperity to everyone.

It looked good in theory, but there were some serious immediate effects.

Raising interest rates choked off economic growth, causing workers to lose their jobs. When governments slashed their budgets, benefits to the poor and unemployed were cut and public works projects—which kept many people employed—ended.

The result often added to the chaos. Some wondered whether the IMF's technique treated the disease by killing the patient.

The workers who were fired and unable now to support themselves or their families saw the IMF not as a help, but as a bully. In Korea, workers asked sarcastically if IMF stood for "I aM Fired." The Korea Confederation of Trade Unions vowed to call for strikes if companies began layoffs.

In response, the IMF continued to lecture: Keep the markets open, let the banks that made bad loans fail. Let the companies that aren't profitable close. Keep down tariffs, and let the currency rise or fall according to the demands of the market. Balance the budget.

Suharto even dared to say no. He would take the IMF bailout, but on his conditions. Other Asian leaders followed Suharto's lead, closing their borders to currency speculations and raising tariffs to protect their industries. In September 1998, Mahathir bin Mohamad in Malaysia ordered new rules that would require foreign investors to keep their money in Malaysia for at least one year.

"People can no longer stay with the so-called free-market system," said Mahathir bin Mohamad. "They need to take some action that is contrary to the philosophy or the principals of the free market."[6]

The liberalization of Asian economies—globalization—was in full retreat.

The West grew impatient. "Hey, this isn't fantasy island, Mr. Suharto," read a *Time* magazine headline.[7]

But many in Eastern Asia preferred to be on fantasy island rather than with the IMF. Also, the IMF plan didn't seem to work. With the ink barely dry after agreeing to lend South Korea $57 billion, the currency collapsed even further, and the South Korean economy seemed to be in full meltdown.

Then investors began pulling out of another economy—Russia's.

In such a serious time, world leaders seemed unable to exert leadership. At a summit in Russia between President Bill Clinton and Russian president Boris Yeltsin, Clinton was forced to answer questions about his affair with an intern named Monica Lewinsky. Yeltsin, incoherent, was barely able to answer questions at all.[8]

The Aftermath

The Asian crisis, its speed and devastation, showed the world as never before how we all exist in a global economy, one bound so tightly that a collapse in Southeast Asia could have an immediate effect on stock prices halfway around the world in New York City and London.

Journalists, citizens, and government leaders all turned their attention to the global economy and began asking questions about the institutions that were supposed to be guarding and guiding it. American workers, as well as their executives, understood that the rest of the world's prosperity was important to them.

"It is just not credible that the U.S. can remain an oasis of prosperity unaffected by a world that is experiencing greatly increased stress," Alan Greenspan said in a speech at the University of California, Berkeley.[9]

What had happened? What had gone wrong?

The last great economic catastrophe in the century had been the Great Depression of the 1930s. Since then, economists and politicians had worked out methods to ensure that such a depression never happened again.

But none of their precautions and safeguards had worked this time. Worse, the devastated economies had all followed the rules of the new economy, as prescribed by the Western countries and its institutions, the IMF and the World Bank.

Alice H. Amsden, professor of political economy at the Massachusetts Institute of Technology, noted in *The New York Times* that the powerful economies that emerged after World War II prospered in exactly the opposite way the IMF and World Bank advocated.

"In their countries, business and government worked closely together to strengthen domestic industry. Foreign enterprises were discouraged, by deliberate red tape, from entering certain industries, so that national companies could get a head start. State-owned banks lent money at subsidized rates to help local firms acquire the technologies and capital equipment they needed," Amsden wrote, referring to Thailand, South Korea, and Taiwan.

"[But] these measures are now identified as protectionist and unfair," she wrote. "To join the international trading system, nations must now agree to the radical notion of a level playing field and, toward that end, must disallow government intervention in the economy beyond establishing certain minimal norms, like standard accounting procedures and contract law."[10]

In other words, the system was rigged in favor of the richer nations, and the economic crises of the late 1990s made this apparent.

The turmoil of the late 1990s made the IMF and the World Bank examine their own policies, even if they didn't change as some activists wanted them to. The result was the beginning of a new dialogue between global institutions and the protesters who kept gathering in ever-increasing numbers at their meetings.

Mistakes and Resolve

In July 2001, representatives of the world's richest nations met in the ancient maritime city of Genoa, Italy, behind a ring of fences erected by police. Protesters gathered at the fences, where they chanted antiglobalization slogans and lit stacks of tires aflame. The meeting broke down in chaos when the protests grew angrier and police charged the crowds on horseback to restore order. One protester was killed.

Inside, the leaders at the summit continued to express their faith in globalization. "We are determined to make globalization work for all our citizens, especially the world's poor, drawing the poorest countries into the global economy is the surest way to address their fundamental aspirations," they said in a final statement.

But by this time, many at the World Bank and IMF were openly acknowledging that their policies had not worked as they had hoped. Many economies had not made an easy transition to capitalism. Others were drowning in debt and social unrest.

Hundreds of people gathered at the funeral of Carlo Giuliani, a twenty-three-year-old Italian activist who was shot during the protests and riots at the 2001 G-8 summit in Italy. He was the first fatality since the antiglobalization movement began staging protests at world meetings in Seattle in 1999.

In 1999, the Meltzer Commission, an independent study group appointed by Congress, described the World Bank as ineffective and bloated with staff.

"Half its projects are unsuccessful, and the failure rate is even higher in the poorest countries," commission chairman Allan H. Meltzer wrote after the report was released. "The bank's management must stop its current public-relations flimflam and start improving its effectiveness in reducing poverty."

William Easterly, a World Bank economist, took leave to write a devastating critique of the bank and its policies. During more than twelve years at the bank, Easterly had visited slums around the world where bank funds had been used to lift people out of poverty. It was his responsibility to determine whether the money had made any difference. His conclusion is startling.

After spending billions over a period of fifty years, World Bank economists simply do not know how to make a poor economy prosper, he wrote in *The Elusive Quest for Growth,* which was published in 2001.

"What strikes you as you look back over the decades," Easterly wrote, "is this repeated cycle where we've all thought there was one key factor that would transform poor countries into growth economies. At one point, it was family planning. At another, it was education. At another, health care or capital investment or 'adjustment loans.' And none of these have had any sustained effect on economic growth. . . . The genuine success stories, where poor countries have achieved long-term sustained growth, have been pitifully few. And in some of those, it's far from clear that bank aid was a major factor, or even any factor at all."

Easterly was scathing about how the bank reacted when its policies clearly had failed. "The bank has acknowledged that 'mistakes were made' but insisted that 'we understand now. We're changing policies, and from now on things will be different.' But the bank's basic approach doesn't really change in any fundamental way."

Easterly argued that the World Bank measured its success by the number of loans it made. Giving money away is not difficult, he noted. Whether the loans achieve anything, however, is not considered. Worst of all, wrote Easterly, the people who made the wasteful loans are never held accountable.

"If the money is stolen by the local government or otherwise misspent, by the time that awareness dawns on the bank, if it ever does, the bank employee who made the loan is somewhere else. He's moved up or somewhere else in the bureaucracy and is never held to account. So ultimately nobody is responsible for anything."

Another economist at the World Bank told a *Washington Post* reporter that, "No one can be happy with the bank's performance in Africa. The area that's received the highest percentage of bank aid is an obvious basket case. Anyone can see that. Who do they think we're fooling? We've poured millions into Zambia, and the living standard today is half what it was 30 years ago. Realities like that won't just melt away."[1]

Third World Debt

Critics say the leaders of the World Bank and IMF are responsible for giving out billions in loans to corrupt leaders. The leaders, or "elites," then waste or steal the money and the population is left responsible to pay the loans.

More than 80 percent of the $40 billion loaned to Argentina from 1976 to 1983 is unaccounted for. The receipts simply don't exist. Given to a military dictatorship, the money was lost, stolen, or put into wasteful projects. But the debt still exists, and the people of Argentina must pay for it.

Many other nations face a similar dilemma. Loans were made and taken, and the money was spent uselessly or stolen. Today, countries that can't afford to build roads, hospitals, or schools must still make huge payments to pay off their debt.

In Tanzania, nearly one half of the population dies before the age of thirty-five. Tanzania's debt payments to the IMF and World Bank, however, are six times the amount it spends on health care. In Africa, government debt payments to the North—mostly creditors in western Europe and North America—are four times the amount spent on health and education.[2]

In six years between 1990 and 1998, the World Bank and the IMF were taking in more dollars in payments from developing nations than they were giving out.

When a country is unable to pay its debts, it must seek help from the World Bank and the IMF, thus renewing the process. The IMF and World Bank then recommend that the country remake its economy in a way that favors transnational corporations, say antiglobalization activists.

"That is why we have more and more billionaires (in both north and south) and more people falling into poverty (in both north and south)," wrote Kevin Danaher in disgust.

$1 a Day

As the rich get richer, say activists, most of the world continues to live, or try to live, on less than $1 a day.

Washington Post reporter Jon Jeter wrote about a Zambian woman with five children who went every day to a giant market in the city of Maramba. There, she set out a table of plump, red tomatoes and prayed for buyers. If she sold enough tomatoes—seventy-five cents' worth—she could buy two bags of maize meal and feed her children. If not, then they went without.

"If you are a mother," Rose Shanzi told Jeter, "you don't know what suffering is until you have watched your babies go hungry. I have suffered many times."

Eight out of ten of Zambia's 10 million citizens live on less than $1 a day.

Jeter wrote that the nation of Zambia was once virtually socialist, but in 1992 had changed over to the free market economy model pushed by the World Bank and the IMF. The result has not been what planners had hoped.

Bloated, inefficient industries were forced to cut thousands of jobs. Many more industries simply shuttered their doors for good. Factories that once produced clothing couldn't compete with second-hand items shipped in from Europe and the United States.

In the ten years since the economy was turned into a free market, the number of unemployed has skyrocketed. The market where Rose sells her tomatoes has tripled in size as people gather, desperate to sell anything to make a living.

During the day Rose spends with Jeter, she makes ninety-seven cents. "Today we are rich," she says.[3]

A New Message

Blistering criticism. Angry protesters who won't go away. A record of few successes and many failures. In response, the leaders of the IMF and the World Bank have begun to soften their stance, engage with protesters, and even echo the words of their protests.

According to Horst Köhler, managing director of the IMF, globalization will help everyone when the rich countries open their markets to workers of the Third World. Rather than target the IMF, he suggested, protesters should lobby the leaders of their countries, who are responsible for opening or closing their markets.

"We have to tackle the selfishness of wealthy countries," said Köhler. "This is a question of morals."[4]

This kind of language is being repeated in many places of power. Realizing that the protesters can no longer be ignored or scorned, and that their arguments must be addressed, the IMF and the World Bank are taking steps to explain their policies to the public.

The World Bank's headquarters is located on H Street in the heart of downtown Washington, just blocks from the White House. More than nine thousand people with 160 different nationalities work at the World Bank, making it the third largest employer in the city. The side facing Pennsylvania Avenue is a graceful facade of glass and steel.

Caroline Anstey, the chief of media relations at the World Bank, recalled that protesters once tried to scale the ten stories of glass and drape a giant banner from the roof decrying World Bank abuses. They were stopped by security. Instead, passersby today can see banners hung by the World Bank that trumpet its successes. One, fluttering in a winter wind, reads "Defeating River Blindness."

Anstey said that the bank had helped cure river blindness, a disease that ravaged African populations. This kind of project, said Anstey, is more typical of what the World Bank does today in its one hundred field offices around the world.

"We used to be the 'big dam' people," she said. "But that's no longer true. No one is saying we haven't made mistakes. It's whether we learn from them."

In simple terms, the World Bank lends money to groups or projects it believes will help eliminate poverty, explained Anstey. The World Bank, she noted, is the largest lender for education in the world, and this kind of statistic shows the bank's new attitude.

"Most of us feel that the critics of the bank are stuck," said Anstey. "They are 10 years old. The bank is not saying 'globalization is good for you.' Globalization has many benefits, but unless it helps the poor, it won't work."

This, said Anstey, has become the World Bank's primary message.

"I think recently we've realized that rich countries have to do more," she said. "The rich countries must open their markets to poorer countries and their cheaper products, and it will be the World Bank who tells them so.

"The bank sees itself as standing up for the rights of the poor," she said. "The young people only get one half of the coin. You have to dismantle the trade barriers."

The bank does not represent the interests of the wealthy, said Anstey. "We're owned by 183 nations," she said.

Anstey said that rich and poor nations have different attitudes and want different things. The rich nations usually want more "transparent markets," which makes it easier to invest in a country, such as building factories and employing local workers. The rich nations are less worried about reaching out to environmental and labor groups—called nongovernmental organizations, or NGOs—even if these groups criticize them. In North American and European politics, NGOs have been around for decades.

But in poor nations, NGOs are often used as a cover by political opponents to attack the government in power, said Anstey. Some government leaders believe NGOs have no right to voice their opinions in the first place. One South African finance minister complained at a World Bank meeting that he was elected by the people of South Africa to represent their interests, not to bow to a mob of people shouting and throwing stones in the street.

Selecting a Project

As part of the process of selecting a project, the bank's field offices talk to the government and ask it what it needs. The people in the offices then come up with a project and a proposal. After being prepared, the proposal is submitted to the World Bank and is voted on by a board of twenty-four nations. The board is usually made up of finance ministers from the twenty-four nations. The board considers whether the proposal will work, whether it will reduce poverty, whether it considers social safeguards.

"Everything is looked at," said Anstey. The bank considers projects that other banks wouldn't; she added, "we go where the private sector won't go."

About 40 percent of the proposals never make it to the board. Some proposals pit the needs of the local people against NGOs in North America. In Chad and Cameroon, the World Bank debated whether to fund an oil pipeline. NGOs in North America bitterly criticized the project, saying it subsidized corporations and would lead to pollution. But local groups decided that the pipeline would offer jobs and an escape from poverty.

Among the bank's goals is seeing that everyone in the world receives primary education, both boys and girls. "We're talking about training teachers, providing buildings," said Anstey. About 120 million children today never receive schooling.

This process has not been without its problems. In one African country, the World Bank bought textbooks for schools. But when a World Bank representative showed up at the school, she found the textbooks still wrapped up in plastic, unopened, and left stacked in a corner. When asked why, the teachers explained that the textbooks were too advanced for even the teachers. The bank realized that it had to educate teachers as well.

The World Bank has also launched programs to convince parents that it is worth educating their girls, said Anstey. One of the critical parts of this program was simple—most schools had only boys' bathrooms. The World Bank has since funded the building of girls' bathrooms in schools. A simple but profound problem with an easy solution, and it represents how the bank is trying to think differently than it has in the past, Anstey claimed.

"Globalization can be a powerful force of good but it has to work for the poor," said Anstey. "The countries that seal themselves off will be left behind. We want globalization with a human face."5

A Debate Changed

The World Bank and the IMF were scheduled to have summit meetings in Washington, D.C., in September 2001. Thousands of protesters also planned to attend. City police braced themselves for what would be a long week of protests and marches.

But then something else happened, something so shocking and horrible that the meetings were canceled and the debate about globalization changed forever. Thomas Friedman's foretelling of the dangers of the "angry man syndrome" came terrifyingly true.

chapter ten

A New World

On the morning of September 11, 2001, a group of nineteen terrorists used box cutters to hijack four passenger planes, two from Boston and two from New York. They steered the first two into the towers of the World Trade Center in New York City. A third plane slammed into the Pentagon in Washington, D.C., exploding in a giant fireball that rose above the city. The fourth airplane was over Pennsylvania and headed toward Washington when the passengers revolted. After a brief struggle, the plane crashed into a field in central Pennsylvania, leaving no survivors.

The 110-story World Trade Center towers burned fiercely. Less than a few hours after the impacts, the structures collapsed, imploding in a thundering cloud of glass, debris, and pulverized concrete. By the end of September 11, around three thousand people had been killed, and the nation seethed in horror, sorrow, and rage.

In the White House, President George W. Bush announced a war on terror.

For many antiglobalization activists, the
destruction of the World Trade Center during the terrorist attacks
of September 11, 2001, proved their point. Activists
considered the attacks to be a reaction against the
ruthless powers of globalization that had
swept aside local cultures and economies.

Reaction

The terrorist attacks that destroyed the World Trade Center and damaged the Pentagon changed the world. They also inspired passionate new debates over globalization. For many activists, the attacks proved their point.

"The entire view of the world that supported the markets' faith in globalisation has melted down," said John Gray, a professor at the London School of Economics, in *The Economist* magazine. "Led by the United States, the world's richest states have acted on the assumption that people everywhere want to live as they do. As a result, they failed to recognise the deadly mixture of emotions—cultural resentment, the sense of injustice and a genuine rejection of western modernity—that lies behind the attacks on New York and Washington."

But not everyone agreed. *The Economist* reacted to Gray's words. "Is there no limit to the crimes for which globalisation must be held to account?" asked one editorial. *The Economist* listed the number of ills now attributed to globalization—destruction of democracy and the environment, Third World poverty.

"Truly," the editorial continued, "the idea that people should be left free to trade with each other in peace must be the most wicked and dangerous doctrine ever devised."[1]

After the attacks, European activists vowed to continue to march against globalization, but the mood was more somber in the United States. The country simply would not tolerate violent, noisy protest after such a tragedy. American activists took a decidedly lower profile. John Sellers, director of the Ruckus Society, told *The New York Times* that the antiglobalization message would be lost at a protest if a few members of the group burned an American flag.[2]

President Bush didn't make things better, according to the activists. Though he acknowledged a link between terrorism and the frustration felt in parts of the world, he declared a probusiness policy to be the solution. He negotiated with Congress to get "fast track" authority, which would allow him to conclude trade agreements quickly and with minimal debate. Antiglobalization groups and unions accused Bush of using the terrorist attacks to promote his probusiness agenda.

A Global Recession

Also, the American economy began to slow down. There had been many signs that the economy had slipped into recession by summer 2001, but the September 11 attacks were an effective exclamation mark. After that, no one seriously doubted that rough economic times were ahead.

The U.S. economic downturn was startling, not only for the sudden descent, but because the rest of the world followed so swiftly. If there was any question about how globalization had linked the rest of the world together, the recession that began in 2001 effectively answered it.

As Europeans watched the slowdown of the American economy, few of them were concerned. Europe, they reasoned, was insulated from the downturn. Some analysts even predicted that Europe would replace the United States as the world's engine of growth.

But that didn't happen. Forty percent of the world's economic growth in the past five years was generated by the United States. The growth in trade had made all nations more interdependent.

Multinational corporations responded to falling profits by cutting jobs. Many of these cuts occurred outside the companies' home country. Fujitsu, a troubled Japanese electronics firm, cut 16,400 jobs, most of them outside Japan. The first sign of European trouble was in Germany, where growth slowed as dramatically as it had in the United States. Unemployment stayed stubbornly high.

As the world slipped into recession, some suggested that the WTO call off its meeting, planned to occur in the Middle Eastern country of Qatar in November. But that suggestion was brushed aside. The delegates arrived, even more determined to make progress than before.

One of the major breakthroughs at Qatar was the admission of both China and Taiwan into the WTO, bringing the organization's membership to 144 members. For China, a Communist country that had embraced capitalism over the past two decades, the admission was especially momentous. China would be able to increase its trade with the capitalist nations, but it would also open up the Chinese market of 1.3 billion consumers to foreign companies. For transnational companies, who had been waiting for access to the Chinese market for decades, the timing could not have been better.

But there were also threats to globalization. The *Wall Street Journal* noted that another period of globalization had been cut short in 1914 by the start of World War I. It took fifty years for global trade to reach 1914 levels again. Some worried that the September 11 attacks would have a similar chilling effect.[3]

The numbers indicated that globalization had stalled. The IMF estimated that growth in global trade slowed from 12 percent in 2000 to just 1 percent in 2001, the slowest rate of growth since 1982.

The Meaning of September 11

As the economy tried to recover from the shock of the attacks, the government was also facing up to what the terrorist attacks meant. About six months after the World Trade Center was destroyed, Vice Admiral Thomas R. Wilson told a congressional committee that the men who flew the planes into the World Trade Center and Pentagon were in a death struggle with globalization:

> The "Post Cold War" period ended on 11 September. The next decade or so may well be defined by the "struggle over globalization." Values and concepts long-championed by the United States and the West—political and economic openness, democracy and individual rights, market economics, international trade, scientific rationalism, and the rule of law—are being carried forward on the tide of globalization— money, people, information, technology, ideas, goods and services are moving around the globe at higher speeds and with fewer restrictions. Our adversaries increasingly understand this link. They equate globalization to Americanization and see the U.S. as the principal architect and primary

beneficiary of an emerging order that undermines their values, interests, beliefs, and culture. They blame the U.S. for "what's wrong" in the world, and seek allies among states, groups, and individuals who worry about U.S. hegemony and are unhappy with the present or perceived future. They are adept at using globalization against us— exploiting the freer flow of money, people, and technology . . . attacking the vulnerabilities presented by political and economic openness . . . and using globalization's "downsides" (demographic and economic imbalances, large numbers of unemployed youth, Western cultural penetration, declining living standards, corrupt and ineffective governments, decaying infrastructures, etc.) to foster an extremist message, and attract recruits and support from among "globalization's losers."

The 11 September terrorist attacks were the first strategic strikes in a war against the U.S. vision of the future world order. They targeted our homeland, but also struck a blow against global openness, the global transportation network, and the global economy. These extremists and their allies understand that their desired world cannot coexist with our brand of globalization. Encouraging, furthering and consolidating the positive aspects of globalization, while reducing and managing its downsides, defeating its enemies, may well be the civilized world's "measure of merit" for the next decade.

Wilson explained that "globalization's losers" were determined to bring the world system down.

"Make no mistake, we are the target. Our adversaries believe they must derail the emerging world order or be overcome by it. They also understand the singular importance of the United States in shaping that order and know that they cannot prevail if the U.S. remains actively engaged and influential around the globe."[4]

The World Economic Forum

The debates over globalization went on. On a cold, wet February day in 2002, hundreds of workers gathered outside the Gap store on Fifth Avenue in New York City. They were mostly from the union AFL-CIO, and they gathered on the sidewalk and lifted signs demanding that Gap pay a living wage.

The workers were gathering to protest during the World Economic Forum, which was usually held in Davos, Switzerland, but had switched to New York City as a sign of solidarity after the World Trade Center was destroyed.

The Davos meeting is normally an exclusive affair, a place where billionaires hobnob with government leaders. The issues of the outside world—especially those chanted by thousands of protesters—were rarely considered by those who held so much power. But this year was different.

Perhaps because of the attacks, or perhaps because of the attention the protesters had finally won from the public, the World Economic Forum had dozens of workshops about globalization. More than 2,700 academics, journalists, politicians, and business leaders participated in panels entitled, "Understanding Global Anger,"

"Bridging the Digital Divide," and "The Politics of Apology."[5]

On one panel, Jack Greenberg, the chairman and CEO of McDonald's, sat next to Amr Moussa, the often very critical secretary-general of the League of Arab States. The two discussed the sources of global rage. Greenberg even commented that the French rage at McDonald's was misdirected.

"All of our buns," he told the audience in one of the panel's lighter moments, "are French."[6]

The discussion was part of a general mood shift away from celebrating globalization to discussing why it had caused such an angry backlash.

Bono, the singer of the rock band U2, shakes hands with Desmond Tutu, Nobel Peace Prize winner of South Africa, during a panel discussion called "For Hope" at the World Economic Forum in February 2002.

"For a couple of years Davos was dominated by the global financial crisis, then two years ago it was the New Economy. Now, after major demonstrations at major economic meetings in the past year or two, there are these profound questions about globalization—how does it work? What is it? What is its impact?" asked Daniel Yergin, chairman of Cambridge Energy Research Associates and one of the panel leaders.[7]

There were some unusual sights. Bono, the lead singer for the rock band U2, who referred to himself as a "spoiled rotten rock star," sat down next to Bill Gates, the billionaire computer genius.

Bono observed in another panel that there was "a desire for the need to believe that the developed world is really interested in the developing world, and we have to prove that."

"We are debating in a very casual setting issues that affect real lives," Bono said. "Discussing barbaric things is itself barbaric. That's why people get annoyed with the World Economic Forum."[8] What is needed, he said, is "real action."

The Treasury Secretary and the Rock Star

To demonstrate "real action," Bono invited U.S. Treasury Secretary Paul O'Neill on a trip to Africa to see firsthand what poverty and aid meant. To the surprise of many, O'Neill accepted. In May 2002, they were off.

They were a strange and unlikely pair. One wore crisp business suits, was one of the most powerful men in the U.S. government, and had run a company worth tens of millions of dollars. The other sported wraparound blue shades and sparkling diamond earrings, and had a musical career worth tens of millions of dollars. But for ten days in Africa, they were together—O'Neill and Bono. They toured spots afflicted with poverty and argued openly about how to solve it. They observed villages of mud huts and cities where thousands suffered from disease or died in the streets.

Through their discussions and perspectives, they debated the basic dilemma that faces globalization today. What is the solution to global poverty—trade or aid?

Bono had already spent time in Africa. In 1984, Bono had performed in two rock shows—Live Aid and Band Aid—that were dedicated to raising funds for the starving in Africa. Afterward, Bono did something few of the other stars did: He went to Africa to see it for himself.

Bono and his wife spent six weeks at an orphanage. In the morning, he would leave his tent and see the bodies of dead and abandoned children. "Or worse," he recalled. "The father of a child would walk up to you and try to give you his living child and say, 'You take it, because if this is your child, it won't die.'"

After his experience, Bono was convinced that lasting solutions had to be found for Africa's problems—which included famine, poverty, civil war, and an exploding number of AIDS infections.

Bono took the issues very seriously, examining both sides and not settling for an easy answer. He met with economists and politicians and gained a reputation as being passionate, thoughtful, and considerate.

In the 1990s, Bono met with Treasury Secretary Lawrence Summers, then under President Bill Clinton. After the meeting, Summers spoke to Clinton.

"You know, some guy just came in to see me in jeans and T-shirt, and he just had one name," said the secretary to Clinton. "But he sure was smart. Do you know anything about him?"

Bono became a spokesman for various aid organizations and championed the removal of Africa's debts—which he said were strangling African health care, school systems, and economies.

When George W. Bush became president, Bono didn't rule out convincing the Republicans of the need to send aid to Africa. The Republicans traditionally have been opposed to foreign aid because it never seems to actually work as intended. Bono made an appointment with Treasury Secretary O'Neill.

"I refused to meet him at first," recalled O'Neill. "I thought he was just some pop star who wanted to use me." But O'Neill did settle for a thirty-minute talk with Bono. The conversation lengthened to ninety minutes, and O'Neill was convinced that Bono was sincere.

"He's a serious person. He cares deeply about these issues, and you know what? He knows a lot about them," said O'Neill.9

The two spent ten days in Africa. To O'Neill, the problem wasn't one of money, but about using it properly. O'Neill recalled that after fifty years and billions in aid, most African nations still struggle with immense problems in health and poverty.

"As Bono, my friend and traveling companion, might say, we still haven't found what we're looking for," O'Neill said in a speech, referring to the lyrics of one of U2's biggest hits.

In May 2002, Bono (left) and U.S. treasury secretary Paul O'Neill talk to the press in Soweto, South Africa, where the U.S. Agency for International Development helped fund the building of new houses for local families.

Bono, who understands this issue, said that, nonetheless, rich countries, and especially the United States, have to give more. "[O'Neill] has a very big wallet. It's not his; he has the United States's wallet," Bono said.

To make his point, Bono took O'Neill to places where aid had decidedly made a difference. They toured a project in the South African township of Soweto, partially funded by the U.S. Agency for International Development, that has enabled thousands of families to leave their shacks made from scrap metal and move into newly built houses.[10]

In return, O'Neill took Bono to the offices of a U.S.-based computer company that employed nine hundred Ghanaians to enter data from American health insurance forms. The employees earned two to four times the nation's average daily wage of about thirty-four cents.

Bono agreed that the jobs were helpful, though he still wasn't sure if multinational corporations were the solution to pulling Africa out of poverty. But "it was clear the workers were very, very happy," he said.

The two men, despite being so different, seemed to get along easily in Africa. They traded jokes and poked fun at each other at various stops. When O'Neill and Bono donned striped African robes and caps presented to them by the chief of a Ghanaian village, O'Neill told Bono, "We're never going to live this down." Bono spoke with mock indignation at the chuckling villagers: "Anyone laughs, there's no more debt cancellation."

O'Neill was clearly stunned by some sights, especially dirty water supplies. The water could be easily cleaned, preventing thousands of deaths from disease, he noted. In a northern Ghanaian village, he observed people drinking water that "looks like rinse water from a washing machine," he said.[11]

After ten days of tours, the pair came to their last stop in Ethiopia. O'Neill pledged that the Bush administration would take a closer look at poverty.

"If you were on this trip with us, and you weren't affected by what we saw," O'Neill told reporters, "you're a piece of wood or something."[12]

The Future of Globalization

No one can predict whether globalization will be effectively addressed and, if it is, what form it will be in. What is certain is that the questions of globalization—economic, political, cultural—will only grow more important in the coming years.

Today, the friction between nations and peoples as the world draws closer together is palpable. The source of that friction must be addressed. The world's leaders, it seems, realize this. They recognize that the promises of globalization have not been delivered everywhere.

In March 2002, world leaders gathered in Monterrey, Mexico, to discuss plans to fight global poverty. Since the fall of the Soviet Union in 1989, capitalism has spread around the world. And yet more people are poor than ever before.

"Rather than an unstoppable force for development, globalization now seems more like an economic temptress, promising riches but often not delivering," observed *New York Times* reporter Joseph Kahn.

President Bush has increased foreign aid by 50 percent to $15 billion, which he hopes will combat some of the slums where terrorists have been successfully recruited.[13] Some wonder whether this aid will cause meaningful change. They claim history has shown that it has not. They argue that aid is invariably stolen or abused. At most, the money props up ineffective rulers, leaving a nation's population without any benefit.

But this time will be different, said Kjell Magne Bondevik, Norway's prime minister. "We know what works, and what doesn't."[14]

The time, however, for determining "what works and what doesn't" has grown short. With the terrorist attacks and environmental breakdown, the stakes have become far higher.

We stand on a "hinge of history," a time that promises to be very different from everything that has gone before. It is a terrifying, awesome, and potentially great moment.

Globalization, which seems to separate so many people and cause so much rage, is also pulling everyone closer together. Perhaps in this lies the solution. The technology of globalization has allowed people throughout the world, for the first time in history, to truly see and to talk to each other. In this communication they may recognize and understand the things that make us all human. It is not difficult to believe, once this recognition takes place, that we will work together to solve the problems that face us.

Source Notes

Chapter 1

1. Kim Murphy, "Groups Evoke an Earlier, Angrier Time," *Los Angeles Times*, December 1, 1999, p. A01.
2. Murphy, p. A01.
3. Jane Bussey and Michael Zielenziger, "WTO Talks Collapse Without Agreement," *San Jose Mercury News*, December 4, 1999, p. A01.
4. David E. Sanger, "Talks and Turmoil: The Overview, President Chides World Trade Body in Stormy Seattle," *The New York Times*, December 2, 1999, p. A01.
5. Thomas Friedman, *The Lexus and the Olive Tree* (New York: Farrar, Straus and Giroux, 1999), p. ix.

Chapter 2

1. P. J. O'Rourke, *Give War a Chance* (New York: Vintage Books, 1993), p. 13.
2. Ken Ringle, "Bank Shot: Writing from the Inside: An Economist Says the World Bank Is Failing Its Mission," *Washington Post,* March 20, 2002, p. C01.

Chapter 3

1. Walter LaFeber, *Michael Jordan and the New Global Capitalism* (New York: W.W. Norton & Company, 1999), p. 60.

2. Paul Krugman, *A Return to Depression Economics* (New York: W.W. Norton & Company, 1999), p. 18.

3. Wayne Ellwood, *The No-Nonsense Guide to Globalization* (Oxford: New Internationalists Publications, Ltd., 2001), p. 55.

4. LaFeber, p. 51.

5. LaFeber, pp. 67–69.

6. Sam Dillion, "Profits Raise Pressures on U.S.-Owned Factories in Mexican Border Zone," *The New York Times,* February 15, 2001, p. A16.

7. William M. Adler, *Mollie's Job: A Story of Life and Work on the Global Assembly Line* (New York: Scribner, 2000), p. 13.

8. Adler, pp. 294–298.

9. Adler, pp. 262–263.

10. Leslie Kaufman and David Gonzalez, "Labor Standards Clash with Global Reality," *The New York Times,* April 24, 2001, p. A01.

11. Interviewed by Danny Schlechter, World Economic Forum, Davos, Switzerland, January 1998, PBS.

12. Yuri Kageyama, "Japan Unemployment Reaches Record High," Associated Press, August 28, 2001.

13. Paul Davies, "Where's the Outrage? Sports World Just Ignores It. Nike Workers' Plight Doesn't Play at Final 4," *Philadelphia Daily News,* March 31, 1997, p. 04.

14. Naomi Klein, *No Logo: Taking Aim at the Brand Bullies* (New York: Picador, 1999), pp. 371–376 and LaFeber, pp. 154–155.

Chapter 4

1. Clive Crook, "Globalization and Its Critics," *Economist,* September 27, 2001.
2. William M. Adler, *Mollie's Job: A Story of Life and Work on the Global Assembly Line* (New York: Scribner, 2000), p. 288.
3. Anthony DePalma, "Talks Tie Trade in the Americas to Democracy," *The New York Times,* April 22, 2001, p. A01.
4. John R. MacArthur, *The Selling of "Free Trade"* (New York: Hill & Wang, 2000), p. 68.
5. Thomas L. Friedman, "Protesting for Whom?" *The New York Times,* April 24, 2002, p. A19.

Chapter 5

1. Michelle Sforza and Lori Wallach, *Whose Trade Organization?* (Washington, D.C.: Public Citizen, 1999), pp. 19–21.
2. H. Josef Hebert, "House Votes to Lift Ban on a Type of Tuna Net," Associated Press, May 22, 1997.
3. Bill McKibben, "A Special Moment in History," *Atlantic Monthly,* Vol. 281, No. 5, May 1998, p. 55.
4. Andrew C. Revkin, "Large Ice Shelf in Antarctica Disintegrates at Great Speed," *The New York Times,* March 20, 2002, p. A13.

Chapter 6

1. Thomas Sancton, "Super Fries Saboteur," *Time,* Dec. 6, 1999, p. 74.

2. Walter LaFeber, *Michael Jordan and the New Global Capitalism,* (New York: W.W. Norton & Company, 1999), p. 20.
3. Thomas Friedman, *The Lexus and the Olive Tree* (New York: Farrar, Straus and Giroux, 1999), p. 319.
4. Ira Winderman, "The NBA Borders Are Wide Open: Look for a Torrent of Overseas Selections in the Draft," *Sun-Sentinel,* June 23, 2002, p. 14C.
5. Vikram Khanna, "The Arts Should Celebrate Globalization," *Business Times,* April 5, 2002.

Chapter 7

1. Kevin Danaher, personal interview, Hofstra University, November 8, 2001.
2. Tom Redburn, "Honoring, and Paying, All Those Who Serve," *The New York Times,* October 28, 2001, p. C4.
3. Naomi Klein, *No Logo: Taking Aim at the Brand Bullies* (New York: Picador, 1999), p. 350.
4. Klein, p. 362.
5. Kevin Danaher, *10 Reasons to Abolish the IMF & World Bank* (New York: Seven Stories Press, 2001), p. 31.
6. Danaher, p. 35.
7. Danaher, interview.
8. Paul Krugman, "Taking Care of Business," *The New York Times,* October 28, 2001, p. D14.
9. Robert Weissman, "Why We Protest," *Washington Post,* September 9, 2001, p. A21.
10. Bryan Hirsch, interview November 6, 2001.

Chapter 8

1. Paul Krugman, *A Return to Depression Economics* (New York: W.W. Norton & Company, 1999), pp. 38–59.

2. Jack Weatherford, *The History of Money* (New York: Crown Publishers, Inc., 1997), p. 252.

3. Weatherford, 280.

4. Johanna McGeary, "Lost Leaders," *Time*, September 14, 1998, p. 37.

5. Terry McCarthy, "Indonesia Burning," *Time*, May 25, 1998, p. 44.

6. Michael Zielenziger, "Battered Economies Have Asia Doubting the West's Medicine," *The Philadelphia Inquirer*, September 4, 1998, p. A25.

7. Adam Zagorin, "Asian Markets," *Time*, January 19, 1998.

8. McGeary.

9. S. C. Gwynne, "What a Drag!" *Time*, September 14, 1998, p. 26.

10. Alice H. Amsden, "Why Are Globalizers So Provincial?" *The New York Times*, January 31, 2002, p. A25.

Chapter 9

1. Ken Ringle, "Bank Shot: Writing from the Inside, an Economist Says the World Bank is Failing Its Mission," *Washington Post*, March 20, 2002, p. C01.

2. Wayne Ellwood, *The No-Nonsense Guide to Globalization* (Oxford: New Internationalists Publications, Ltd., 2001), p. 51.

3. Jon Jeter, "Less than $1 Means Family of 6 Can Eat," *Washington Post*, February 19, 2002, p. A01.

4. Joseph Kahn, "Fewer Strings Attached, The World's Bankers Try Giving Money, Not Lessons," *The New York Times*, October 1, 2000, p. D5.

5. Caroline Anstey, personal interview, Washington, D.C., December 6, 2001.

Chapter 10

1. *The Economist,* "Is Globalization Doomed?" September 29, 2001.
2. Leslie Wayne, "For Trade Protesters 'Slower, Sadder Songs,'" *The New York Times,* October 28, 2001, p. C01.
3. "Globalization Persists in Precarious New Age," *The Wall Street Journal,* December 31, 2001, p. A01.
4. Vice Admiral Thomas R. Wilson, prepared testimony before Senate Armed Services Committee, March 19, 2002.
5. Michael Powell and Ben White, "A Revolution in Reverse at Economic Forum," *Washington Post,* February 2, 2002, p. A03.
6. Powell and White, p. A03.
7. Serge Schmemann, "Where McDonald's Sits Down with Arab Nationalists," *The New York Times,* February 2, 2002, p. A10.
8. Serge Schmemann, "Global Forum: Sharing Viewpoints," *The New York Times,* February 4, 2002, p. A14.
9. Josh Tyrangiel, "Bono's Mission," *Time,* February 23, 2002.
10. Paul Blustein, "Good Spirits Despite Difference," *Washington Post,* May 26, 2002, p. A24.
11. Blustein, A24.
12. Paul Blustein, "Treasury Bonds with Bono," *Washington Post,* June 4, 2002, p. C01.
13. Joseph Kahn, "Buying Friends or Building Nations?" *The New York Times,* March 24, 2002, p. D05.
14. Paul Blustein, "The Right Aid Formula This Time Around?" *Washington Post,* March 24, 2002, p. A27.

Bibliography

Adler, William M. *Mollie's Job: A Story of Life and Work on the Global Assembly Line.* New York: Scribner, 2000.

Buchholz, Todd G. *From Here to Economy: A Shortcut to Economic Literacy.* New York: Plume Books, 1996.

Danaher, Kevin. *10 Reasons to Abolish the IMF & World Bank.* New York: Seven Stories Press, 2001.

Ellwood, Wayne. *The No-Nonsense Guide to Globalization.* Oxford: New Internationalists Publications, 2001.

Epping, Randy Charles. *A Beginner's Guide to the World Economy.* New York: Vintage Books, 1992.

Greider, William. *One World, Ready or Not: The Manic Logic of Capitalism.* New York: Simon & Schuster, 1997.

Hutton, Will, and Anthony Giddens, eds. *Global Capitalism.* New York: The New Press, 2000.

Klein, Naomi. *No Logo: Taking Aim at the Brand Bullies.* New York: Picador, 1999.

Krain, Matthew, Howard D. Mehlinger, and Patrick O'Meara, eds. *Globalization and the Challenges of a New Century: A Reader.* Indianapolis: Indiana University Press, 2000.

Krugman, Paul. *A Return to Depression Economics.* New York: W.W. Norton & Company, 1999.

LaFeber, Walter. *Michael Jordan and the New Global Capitalism.* New York: W.W. Norton & Company, 1999.

MacArthur, John R. *The Selling of "Free Trade."* New York: Hill & Wang, 2000.

O'Rourke, P. J. *Give War a Chance.* New York: Vintage Books: 1993.

Soros, George. *George Soros on Globalization.* New York: PublicAffairs, 2002.

Weatherford, Jack. *The History of Money.* New York: Crown Publishers, 1997.

For More Information

Books

Bookbinder, Steven. *The Dictionary of the Global Economy.* Danbury, CT: Franklin Watts, 2001.
A reference book for young adults containing terms and definitions of the global economy.

Buchholz, Todd G. *From Here to Economy.* New York: Penguin Books, 1995.
This is a highly readable—and often fun—account of the forces that drive the national and world economies.

Fridell, Ron. *Education For All: Floating Schools, Cave Classrooms, and Backpacking Teachers.* Brookfield, CT: Twenty-First Century Books, 2003.
This book explains what NGOs are doing to provide education to children and adults around the world.

Fridell, Ron. *The War on Hunger: Dealing with Dictators, Deserts, and Debt.* Brookfield, CT: Twenty-First Century Books, 2003.
This book discusses what governments and NGOs are doing around the world to fight starvation.

Friedman, Thomas. *The Lexus and the Olive Tree*. New York: Farrar Straus Giroux, 1999.
Friedman writes from his perspective as a *New York Times* columnist on globalization and how he believes it forces changes mainly for the better.

Gay, Kathlyn. *Who's Running the Nation?: How Corporate Power Threatens Democracy*. Danbury, CT: Franklin Watts, 1998.
A clear and concise survey of how corporations use their power to influence government.

Krain, Matthew, Patrick O'Meara, and Howard D. Mehlinger, eds. *Globalization and the Challenges of a New Century*. Bloomington: Indiana University Press, 2000.
An excellent collection of writings on globalization from social, political, and economic perspectives.

Web sites

50 Years Is Enough: U.S. Network for Economic Justice
www.50years.org/index.html
A partisan site dedicated to stopping the IMF, the World Bank, and current globalization.

International Forum on Globalization
www.ifg.org/
A site that is "an alliance of sixty leading activists, scholars, economists, researchers, and writers formed to stimulate new thinking, joint activity, and public education in response

to economic globalization." This site is critical of the World Bank and IMF and the current state of globalization.

International Monetary Fund
www.imf.org
The IMF's homepage contains summaries, information, and news on its programs and policies.

The United Nations
www.un.org
The homepage of the UN includes a search engine to look up information on globalization and how it is perceived around the world.

The World Bank
www.worldbank.org
Like the IMF's Web site, the World Bank's homepage offers reports, information, and news releases on its projects.

Note from the author: Globalization is unfolding in so many ways and so quickly, that it can be followed only by reading newspapers and magazines, or by watching high-quality television news every day. Fortunately, most newspapers and magazines are accessible over the Internet. Many of them are free. I recommend *The Wall Street Journal, The New York Times,* and the *Washington Post.* I also try to read *Time, Newsweek, The Economist,* and *Business Week* whenever I can.

Index

about the author

Brendan January is an award-winning author of more than twenty-five books for young readers. He is a graduate of Haverford College in Pennsylvania and Columbia Graduate School of Journalism in New York City. In 2002, January was awarded a Fulbright Scholarship to study the Euro and the integration of Europe.